# A BETTER WAY TO LIVE

## 60 Tips for Life

### BARRY PHILLIPS

Published by
Knowledge Is King
Mortimer House
49 Church Street
Theale
RG7 5BX
United Kingdom

Telephone 01491 201530
Email sales@knowledgeisking.co.uk
www.knowledgeisking.co.uk

A Better Way To Live
ISBN 978-1-7397139-0-4

I dedicate this book to
Asa, Reannon, Lyle, Lyla and Mya.

You inspired me to write this book.
I love you all so much.
Thank you for being just the way you are.

# A BETTER WAY TO LIVE

# INTRODUCTION

*W*e all have a story to tell, whether we publish it to share with the world, or keep it just for ourselves or our family.

I feel the above statement encapsulates exactly what this book is and why I decided to put pen to paper. As I approached my sixtieth birthday, I wanted to share my story and the key life-changing tips that had shown me "A better way to live". I also wanted to honour turning sixty; I was so glad I'd lived long enough to say those words and celebrate their meaning. I have turned sixty; I'm alive, healthy and strong.

I have been blessed to have worked in the personal development arena for the past twenty-five years, running a company that has sold over a million life-changing books. Originally the idea was just to write these life-changing tips as a kind of legacy for my three wonderful children and my two adorable grandchildren. However, as I started to collect them all up and write them down, I decided to share them in my blog mainly to see what feedback I would get. The response from my blog audience has been phenomenal and is the reason you now hold this book in your hands! Thank you to **everyone** who said, "You should put your blogs into a book!"

My intention with this book is to share my top tips with you in the hope that some of them may "speak to you" and allow you to live a better life. This book is not really about me, but about what you hear as you read it. I want you to imagine that we are out walking on a star-filled night. I tell you about a specific star and I point to it with my index finger, but if you keep looking at my finger, you are not going to see the star. When you read my book, don't listen to my words, my words are like my finger. The star I am pointing you towards is your **inner wisdom**.

As you read through the book, you will see there is no real order to the subjects, or the way to read it. Some of you will read it page by page, some will be attracted to specific titles and others will just open it up randomly. The only thing that matters is what you see and hear.

# 1

## START AFRESH

*I*t's never too late to become who you want to be. I hope you live a life that you're proud of, and if you find that you're not, I hope you have the strength to start afresh. We can choose to start afresh in this very moment; there is no need to wait for a new year or a new month or a new week.

There are times in our lives that lend themselves to starting something new. The beginning of a new year, leaving a job, moving home, starting an exciting new book – these all are times that turn our minds to fresh starts. Their advantage is that they bring with them the energy of that event, creating a tide of change around them that we can ride to our next shoreline. But we can choose to start afresh anytime. In any moment we can decide that a bad day or a relationship that's got off on the wrong foot can be started again. It is a mental shift that allows us to clean the slate and approach anything with fresh eyes, and we can make that choice at any time.

Starting afresh is most powerful when we focus our attention on what we are choosing to create. Setting an intention helps us to live our lives the way we want to live them. It's not an expectation that things will go perfectly, but simply a setting of intention.

Giving all of our attention to the unwanted aspects of our lives allows what we resist, to persist. We need to remember to leave enough room in the process of new beginnings to be kind to ourselves, because it takes time to become accustomed to anything new, no matter how much we like it. There is no need to be down on ourselves if we don't reach our new vision instantly. Instead, we can acknowledge the forward motion and choose to reset and start again, knowing that with each choice we learn, grow, and move forward.

Making the choice to start afresh has its own positive energy. Once the journey has begun, it may take unexpected turns, but it never really ends. Like cycles in nature, there are periods of obvious growth and periods of dormancy. Each time we choose to start afresh, we create a better way to live.

*"If you want your life to be a magnificent story,*
*then begin by realising that you are the author,*
*and each day you have the opportunity to write a new page."*

*Mark Houlahan*
*Author*

# 2

## ATTITUDE REALLY IS EVERYTHING

*T*here is no secret recipe for happiness and contentment. The individuals who move through life joyously have not necessarily been blessed with lives of abundance, love, success, and prosperity. Such people have, however, been blessed with the ability to take the circumstances they've been handed and make them into something great.

Our individual realities are coloured by perception – delight and despair come from within rather than outside. Situations we regard as fortuitous please us, while situations we judge as unfavourable cause us no end of grief. Yet if we can look at all we have accomplished without dwelling on our perceived misfortune and make each new circumstance our own, the world as a whole becomes a brighter place. A simple shift in attitude can help us recognise and unearth the hidden potential for fulfilment in every event, every relationship, every duty, and every setback.

The universe is often an unpredictable and chaotic place, and the human tendency is to focus on the negative. But life can be no more or no less than what you make of it. If you are working in a job you dislike, try to concentrate on the positive aspects of the position and approach your work with enthusiasm. What can you do with this job that can turn it around to make it enjoyable? When faced with the prospect of undertaking a task you fear, you can view it as an opportunity to discover what you are truly capable of doing. Similarly, unexpected events, when viewed as surprises, can add flavour to your existence. By choosing to love life no matter what crosses your path, you can create an atmosphere of joy that is wonderfully infectious. An attitude of acceptance is all it takes to change your world.

To make a conscious decision to be happy is not enough. Learn to observe life's complexities through the eyes of a child, seeing everything for the first time. You must furthermore divest yourself of preconceived notions of what is good and what is bad, so that you can appreciate the rich insights concealed in each stage of your life's journey. Learn to discover the joy of wanting what you have.

When you extend unconditional love to everyone, that is an attitude of kindness. When you send good wishes to those who are in deep sorrow, that is an attitude of mercy. When you see the good rather than the weaknesses in people, that is an attitude of compassion. When you bless and uplift someone even as they slander you, that is an attitude of forgiveness.

When you tolerate a situation and take responsibility as well as give cooperation, even when not appreciated, that is an attitude of service.

It has taken me a long time to truly understand the saying "It's not what happens to you, it's how you respond to it that matters." Every moment of your life is nurtured by attitude. When you change the way you look at things, the things you look at change.

*"Things turn out best for those
who make the best of the way things turn out."*

*Art Linkletter (1912-2010)
Canadian radio and television personality*

# 3

## BE THE CHANGE YOU WISH TO SEE

*"I was neurotic for years. I was anxious and depressed and selfish. Everyone kept telling me to change. I resented them, and I agreed with them, and I wanted to change, but simply couldn't, no matter how hard I tried. Then one day someone said to me, 'Don't change. I love you just as you are.' Those words were music to my ears: I relaxed. I came alive. And suddenly I changed!"*

*Anthony De Mello (1931-1987)*
*Spiritual teacher and writer*

The only way to create change is not to try to convince others to change, but to change ourselves. We all know from experience that we can't change other people, yet despite years of trying and failing to change others, most of us have a tendency to continue to try. This is because we naturally feel the need to do something to change situations that we find troubling. When we make adjustments from within, we become role models for others; leading by example is much more inspiring than a lecture or an argument.

We sometimes look outside ourselves for what's wrong with the world, but the outside world is really just a mirror reflecting us back to ourselves. When we encounter negativity – anger, depression, fear – we empower ourselves by looking for its roots inside of ourselves. For example, if you have a friend who is unreliable, observe yourself and notice if there are ways in which you are unreliable. You may be surprised to discover that you have your own struggles with this issue in ways you weren't able to see. Once you own the issue for yourself, you can begin to work on change within yourself. This will also enable you to have more compassion for your friend. At the very least, as you strive to become more reliable, you will become more of the person you want to be. In the best-case scenario, you will be an inspiration to others as you become the change you wish to see.

You can apply the same method to larger issues. For example, if there is something you see in the larger world that you would like to change – let's say violence – try taking responsibility for changing it in yourself. Instead of being angry with those you see as violent, seek out the roots of your own violent thoughts, words and actions, and come to terms with your power to transform them. When we practice non-violence, it means never hurting others even through our thoughts and words. Most of us make a great effort not to hurt people physically, but sometimes we hurt others through our words, often accidentally.

Decide to really think about the consequence of your words before you speak and consider how they might hurt others. In addition, notice how when we do express negativity, it makes those around us feel negative, which in turn affects us for the worst too. This may be the best way to lead the world toward greater understanding and acceptance of each other, which ultimately leads to the peace we all desire.

True freedom is always about changing ourselves. The changes we seek are not outside but within ourselves – beauty, truth, peace, happiness. We have everything we need within.

*"I alone cannot change the world,*
*but I can cast a stone across the waters to create many ripples."*

*Mother Teresa (1910-1997)*
*Nun and missionary*

# 4

## GENUINE PEOPLE SKILLS

*A*s I made the transition from teenager to adult, I started to recognise the importance of people skills. Understanding people and human nature allows us to truly connect with others. We connect with people when we become genuinely interested in them.

When we are genuinely interested, we become curious and ask questions, for example: "How is your family?", "Do you have kids?", "How long have you been with the company?", "Is this your home town?", "What are your hobbies?", "Where did you go on holiday recently?", "What team do you follow?" Most of us are not effective with questions because we are too busy thinking and talking about ourselves. When we genuinely listen to others, we find out what really matters to them.

Understand that the most universal trait of humankind is the desire to be important, the desire to be recognised, to be seen, and to belong. When we genuinely make people feel this way, they will respond to us.

Listed below are some of the key people skills that have helped me to live a better life. If you want to deepen your understanding of skills with people, I strongly recommend *How to Win Friends and Influence People* by Dale Carnegie.

- Listening to people is just about the best way to make anyone feel seen, understood, and important. I feel listening is so important that I have devoted the next chapter to it.

- Give honest, sincere compliments. Recognition and appreciation are basic human needs.

- Find out and use their names whenever possible. Remember that a person's name is to that person the most important sound in any language.

- Pause before you answer them. This acknowledges that you have thought over what they said and that it was worthy of thinking over.

- Acknowledge people who are waiting to see you. If they have to wait, let them know you know they are waiting.

- Pay attention to everybody in a group situation.

- Develop an agreeable nature. Try honestly to see things from the other person's point of view.

*"Getting along well with other people is still*
*the world's most needed skill.*
*With it... there is no limit to what a person can do.*
*We need people; we need the cooperation of others.*
*There is very little we can do alone."*

*Earl Nightingale (1921-1989)*
*American author and radio speaker*

# 5

## THE GIFT OF DEEP LISTENING

### The Deer Hunters

A couple of hunters are out in the woods when one of them falls to the ground.

He doesn't seem to be breathing and his eyes are rolled back in his head.

The other hunter starts to panic, then whips out his cell phone and calls 911.

He frantically blurts out to the operator, "My friend Bubba is dead! What can I do?"

The operator, trying to calm him down, says, "Take it easy. I can help. Just listen to me and follow my instructions. First, let's make sure he's dead."

There's a short pause, and then the operator hears a loud gunshot!

The hunter comes back on the line and says, "OK, now what?"

*S*ometimes, it's easy to hear the words without listening to the real message. We think that we know what's being said, but we don't clarify the situation before jumping to unnecessary and unhelpful conclusions.

In today's high-tech, high-speed, high-stress world of distraction, communication is more important than ever. We crave to be heard and to be seen, yet we seem to devote less and less time to really listening to one another. Genuine listening has become a rare gift. It helps to build lasting relationships, solve problems, ensure understanding and resolve conflicts. At work, effective listening means fewer errors and less wasted time. At home, it helps develop resourceful, self-reliant kids who can solve their own problems. Listening builds friendships and careers. It saves money and marriages.

In fact, being a good listener is one of the most important and enchanting life skills anyone can have. Yet, few of us know how to do it, mainly because no one has taught us how to really listen, as so few have listened sufficiently well to us. So we come to social life greedy to speak rather than listen, hungry to meet others, but reluctant to hear them.

"We have two ears and one tongue so that we would listen more and talk less," said the Greek philosopher Diogenes.

Unfortunately, the majority of us are not good listeners, despite the fact that most of us think we are. Most people don't listen with the intent to understand; they listen with the intent to reply. The truth is we can't think and listen at the same time!

Here are some of the traps we fall into:

- We spend most of our time listening to ourselves rather than to the other person.

- We get distracted by things going on around us.

- We interpret what others say through our own filters, rather than trying to understand what's really going on for them.

- We tune out because we think we already know what someone is going to say, and we may think that what others have to say isn't important.

- We start working out our response rather than hearing them out. Listening is not waiting to talk; listening is listening.

- We quickly judge (we agree or disagree), rather than opening ourselves up to another's point of view; but judgement severely inhibits free conversation.

- We hear the words only and not the deeper needs or meaning conveyed.

- We try to make others feel better by offering solutions and "quick fixes", rather than letting them work through their own experience.

## So just what is Deep Listening?

Have you ever spoken to someone who made you feel like you were the only person in the world at that moment? Who seemed truly engaged and interested in every word you said? How did it make you feel? Did you feel heard, understood, important, valued, and seen? This is the gift of deep listening.

I define deep listening as suspending judgement and being fully present with another person to understand his or her experience or point of view. Deep listening involves hearing more than the words of the speaker and taps into the deeper meaning, unspoken needs, and feelings conveyed. It is something that is done with your heart as well as your mind.

I recently became a Samaritan listener to help others and to become a better listener. One of the many things this role taught me was that listening can be just as powerful as talking when it comes to establishing a connection with another person. People feel valued when they are listened to; it promotes feelings of trust and respect.

Deep listening is transformative. With deep listening, you are not only allowing yourself the time and space to fully absorb what your conversation partner is saying, you are also creating a safe space for them, which allows them to feel heard as they share. This leads to a deeper connection. The only way I can describe my experiences of deep listening is that I feel at one, not just with the other person, but with life.

Do you know anyone who doesn't like to be listened to? There are few more valuable gifts you can give the people in your life than that of a willingness to really listen to them.

# 6

## WHERE WILL YOU LIVE?

$\mathcal{I}$f you don't take care of your body, where are you going to live?

I just love that phrase. It's so simple and true.

We can spend endless hours at work, trying to further our careers so that we can live in nice houses, with comfortable furniture, and lovely interior design, but if we are not taking care of our bodies, we won't be able to enjoy our homes.

We can devote endless energy to accumulating status symbols like cars, jewellery, handbags, exotic holidays, or second holiday homes, but if we are neglecting our health, we may not be able to enjoy them.

We can clamour for attention, win awards and promotions, get recognition, get elected or appointed to important positions, and make ourselves well known, but if our physical form is deteriorating, it may all seem worthless.

It's interesting how most of the major diseases of today are caused by the same things: smoking, diet, being overweight, alcohol and stress.

Here are my top habits of healthy living:

- Get enough sleep
- Drink plenty of water; it's my favourite drink, and it replenishes and refreshes me
- Maintain a healthy weight by eating a balanced diet
- Exercise daily
- Minimise alcohol use
- Don't smoke
- Minimise sugar/salt intake
- Use preventative medicine, like free screenings, nutritional supplements and so on
- Slow down and reduce stress

If you're not already doing some of these things then it might seem like a lot to change, but let me share something with you: I changed all of these in the last decade. I did it, and so can you. I changed one habit at a time, slowly, in tiny steps, and it wasn't hard. Don't try to change everything at once, and don't make it hard on yourself. It's actually easy if you are patient and if you just start.

Here's how to change a habit if you wish to:

Change **one** habit at a time. It doesn't matter which habit you choose. Just choose one. You'll want to do more than one, but don't.

Create positive habits you enjoy. Read the last word again – if you enjoy it, the habit change will be easier. For example, I enjoy walking, so I started to walk every day.

Start as small as possible. Just do a bit the first week, and try to be as consistent as possible. Small change is by far the most effective method I've used for changing habits. Slow change lasts. It helps some people to make it social. They find a partner or group to change the habit with; this way they are more likely to stick with it. These work, and every time I stick to these principles, I've changed a habit.

Healthy living isn't impossible, or even especially difficult. It's just slower to come by than most people care for. Taking care of your body, no matter what, is an investment, and the return is priceless.

# 7

## YOGA AND THE FIVE TIBETANS

*I* was blessed to discover yoga in my late forties. I had been struggling for years with a reoccurring challenge with my lower back, and everyone I turned to for professional help asked me if I "had considered taking up yoga?". Eventually I listened, despite the story in my head that yoga was only for flexible people of mainly the opposite sex to me!

How wrong I was! Yoga has truly shown me a better way to live. It has taken me to some amazing countries and introduced me to lots of beautiful people. At one of the yoga retreats, I was introduced to The Five Tibetan Rites, a ten-minute a day routine that I have practiced most days for over ten years now which have literally changed my life.

The Five Tibetans are an ancient, once-secret anti-ageing ritual of five yoga sequence-like movements that you perform twenty-one repetitions of each a day. They were practiced by Tibetan monks and were discovered in a remote Tibetan monastery by a British Colonel named Colonel Bradford. They are thought to be more than 2,500 years old. What is so remarkable about the Five Tibetans is the way that they exercise and stretch every muscle and articulate every joint with just five short exercises, as well as energising the vital chakra system of energy centres in the body. They are great for all types of people. They are known as a way to reverse many of the physical impacts of aging and are referred to as the Ancient Secret of the Fountain of Youth.

Some writers report benefits that sound too good to be true, but here are some of the benefits I have experienced and what you can truthfully expect:

- Increased energy
- Improved vitality or zest for life
- Reduced stress
- Better sleep
- Improved mental clarity and focus
- Improved breathing
- A stronger body
- Better flexibility
- Increased awareness and mindfulness

In fact, the monks who developed the rites didn't describe specific benefits – they simply stated that the specific purpose of the rites was to regain health, youth and vitality.

I know yoga and the Five Tibetans will not be for everyone, however I strongly encourage anyone to at least try a couple of different forms and classes. My advice to people is to find an accredited yoga teacher to teach you the Five Tibetans. I resisted yoga for so long because of a misunderstanding that I had around it.

I have learned that the goal of yoga is to feel, not to accomplish, and to learn to control the fluctuations of the mind. It's to create space where you were once stuck. To unveil the layers of protection you've built around your heart. To appreciate your body and become aware of the mind and the noise it creates. To make peace with who you are. The goal of yoga is **to love you**.

# 8

## LIVING YOUR LIFE ON PURPOSE

*L*ike me, you might have heard a multitude of stories recently about people handing in their notice in order to find themselves. The pandemic caused people to rethink priorities in life, leading them to the conclusion that they need more meaning and purpose in their work and daily life. One article I read recently said that as many as 40% of all workers had considered leaving their job in 2021. That's a pretty high number!

There's no right or wrong answer when it comes to whether or not someone should leave their job for personal reasons – only what feels right for each individual person in different circumstances. And I'm not here to advocate one way or another. In fact, even if you aren't considering a career change and find a lot of joy in your work, you are probably on some level still feeling some version of this experience where you sometimes ask yourself, "Is this all that there is?"

Whatever camp you happen to fall into, I believe that it is very normal to feel shaky about whether you are on the right path with your work, and to question what your life purpose is, or be uncertain about what you should do next.

We all want to...

- Know what our driving ambitions should be in life
- Feel that we are more than our nine-to-five job
- Experience contentment in our daily routines, and with our loved ones
- Feel that we're on the right path

Let me let you in on a secret: no one is free from this struggle. And your job has nothing to do with it in many cases. Look at the most successful people you can think of – Elon Musk, Bill Gates, Elton John, Tiger Woods, Oprah Winfrey or Taylor Swift. Do you think they have it all figured out? Do you think they have certainty and a feeling of reaching perfection? There's not many of us who feels certainty about their purpose or path.

Most people never feel they've found the perfect job, the perfect productivity routine, the perfect version of themselves ... because it simply doesn't exist. Instead, our ideals about ourselves and the reality we inhabit are constantly not being met, and so we stress out. And it builds up. Because here's the thing... It's often our attachment to the way we want things to be, and our clinging to this ideal that causes us the most suffering. For better or worse, if we can begin to relate differently with this truth, then we also can hold the possibility of shifting our experience towards love for the present moment.

We can begin to notice the stress around our lack of certainty and from this place make a decision about what we want to do next. We can loosen our attachment to having the "perfect plan", and realise that life doesn't have to be one way; in fact, it would be quite boring if we knew exactly what was coming next.

We can get curious about what is in front of us, and be open to the possibility in each moment as it arises. This is what is available to us when we create space to reflect, and it can be beautiful.

The highest purpose is always giving, or serving others, without wanting anything in return. This is why peace of mind is impossible if we are always 'on the take'. There is an overall purpose for your life. Take time to think deeply, listen to your intuition, your inner wisdom, and with patience and in time, the reason why you are here and what you uniquely have to give, will occur to you. Then you can live your life 'on purpose'.

Since life's journey is one of evolution, you may need to redefine your purpose throughout your lifetime. For instance, being an amazing parent may be your life's purpose for eighteen years. Your life's purpose may not be something you are recognised or financially compensated for, such as parenting, a beloved hobby, or a variety of other activities typically deemed inconsequential. Your love for a pursuit, however, gives it meaning.

You'll know you have discovered your life's purpose when you wake up eager to face each day and you feel good about not only what you do, but also who you are.

# 9

## BEING AUTHENTIC

*"When you are authentic, you create a certain energy...
people want to be around you because you are unique."*

Andie MacDowell (1958- )
*American actress*

There's a unique and unmistakable power in knowing, becoming, and being your true self. Those who are truly content in life understand this power and passionately stick to being their authentic selves. To be authentic is not to allow a situation or person to change you, unless for the better. It's being true to yourself, regardless of who is in your company. It's who you truly are at your core. To be your authentic self requires honesty, vulnerability, and courage; it's also incredibly rewarding.

In order to realise and understand who your true self is, you have to start by thinking about your own life. We all get caught up in the trends of wearing the right clothes, driving the right cars, having the latest all-singing, all-dancing phones, and working in the highest paying jobs. Reflect on how striving to fit in with these trends impacts your life. Ask yourself how it makes you feel to be constantly striving for and living inside these trends. Are those things the true you?

Inner reflection can sometimes feel intimidating, but it will help you to discover and get in touch with your authentic self. In his book *The Four Agreements*, Don Miguel Ruiz writes that *"our biggest fear is taking the risk to be alive and express what we really are."* He is absolutely right. If you want to be completely alive and be your authentic self, start your inner reflection by answering these five questions.

1. When you were young, what did you want to be when you grew up? What did you enjoy? Did you have a dream? Most of us got sidetracked from our enjoyment by status, money, responsibility and life. Picture yourself in your childhood dream. Remember that smile and that feeling of positive energy. That feeling and positive energy can be yours whenever you want.

2. What makes you laugh? Laugh at what you find funny. Who cares if the person next to you is laughing? Laughing feels good, makes us happier people and sets us free to enjoy the life we are living. Laughter is a powerful tool that can change your mood and your perception of what is happening in the moment. Enjoy the smile and the feeling of happiness inside of you.

3. What clothes do you feel comfortable in? This is a serious question. It doesn't matter if you like dressing in suits every day or prefer a T-shirt and shorts with no

shoes, wear what makes you comfortable. Clothes are a way of expressing yourself and what you wear should be comfortable and should reflect the true you. Over the years, lots of people have commented on my wearing shorts all year round, but it's what I feel comfortable in.

4. What activities do you really enjoy? Discovering these activities will help guide you towards a place where you want to spend time. By finding and immersing yourself in this place, you will feel happier and more energised.

5. Around whom can you be yourself? We are social creatures by nature, so it is important to spend time with people who make us feel good and accept us for who we really are. When we are with people who do not judge us but accept us, we are able to express our authentic self.

Once you discover who your authentic self is, you will not only feel more content but more at peace and more energised. You have one precious life to live. Spend it following your passions. If you are not passionate about something, follow your curiosity, and your heart. Remember, the only expectations that truly matter are the ones that matter to you.

*"The difference between who you are*
*and who you want to be is what you do."*

*Bill Phillips*
*Fitness pro and author*

# 10

## BE WONDER-FULL

*L*ook out on life with amazement. The variety, the diversity, the manner of every person, the beauty amidst the drudgery, the contrasts, the opportunities, the heroism in the lives of ordinary people, your gifts, your talents, your friends – even just one friend – are all amazing.

When you live life full of wonder, you attract wonderful experiences and people. Don't kill it with cynicism or criticism; don't sabotage your life with moaning and complaining.

Always stay curious and interested. Open the eyes in your head and choose to see the stunning, awesome, diverse beauty of life happening around you right now. I recently started to find joy and reason in mundane tasks; I now know it can shift the flow, and make it not so bad after all. Spending an afternoon working on the car, gardening, or even cleaning the house can be fun when we have an interest in the project. Yet, we can also find joy in the chores and tasks we don't especially like. All we need is a change of attitude, a different way of looking at things, and the tasks or responsibilities that we perceive as tedious can become a source of pleasure.

Most of us tend to put off what we don't want to do. Yet, one of the best approaches to an unpleasant task or dull chore is to dive right in and be fully mindful of what it is that you are doing. You may not perceive washing the shower screen as enjoyable, but it can be if you view it as a loving act for both yourself and your family.

I did this only last week when I hung out my son's washing that he had forgotten was in the washing machine. It's not something I would normally relish but when I thought of it as an act of love towards him, it totally changed the way I felt about it, it actually became pleasurable. When you next pay your bills, thank the universe that you are able to receive the product or service you are paying for. And, each morning, see how neatly you can make your bed and take pride in your results.

Playing your favourite music, dancing while you work, or creating a mental list of everything you are grateful for are just a few ways to turn an unexciting activity into a fun event. Meet it with your heart and you will enrich and be enriched in one single moment.

# 11

## PRACTICE EMPATHY, COMPASSION AND SELF-COMPASSION

### Empathy

*E*mpathy is the ability to understand another person's thoughts and feelings in a situation from their point of view, rather than your own. It differs from sympathy, where one is moved by the thoughts and feelings of another but maintains an emotional distance.

The difference between sympathy and empathy is astutely portrayed in an excerpt from Dr. Brené Brown's TED talk on empathy. She explains that sympathy is to see someone in a deep hole, whilst remaining on higher ground and talking to them from above. The sympathetic person may also try to simply put a silver lining on the other person's situation instead of acknowledging the person's pain. Conversely, empathy is feeling with the person, it's climbing down the hole to sit beside them, being vulnerable to sincerely connect with them. The empathetic person recognises the person's struggle without minimising it.

## Compassion

Compassion helps us connect with others, mend relationships, and move forward while fostering emotional intelligence and well-being. Compassion takes empathy one step further because it harbours a desire for all people to be free from suffering, and it comes with a genuine desire to help.

Compassion is a way to give of ourselves in such an honest and invaluable manner that lifts another. Gestures from the heart, wrapped in an understanding that we are all part of the same human family, is an example of compassion. Everyday examples of compassion aren't hard to accomplish. I find opportunities to have conversations with people in lifts, in stores and whenever the opportunity arises. When I am unable to make conversation verbally, I do it with a smile or eye contact instead. Something that says 'we are the same' and 'I see you and honour your being'. Opening a door, giving up a seat, allowing someone to go ahead of me in a queue, a listening ear with no judgement. There are so many ways to show compassion and when we do so, we demonstrate our love for all humanity.

## Self-compassion

Everyday compassion starts with us. Self-compassion involves treating ourselves the way we would treat a friend who is having a hard time. Individuals who are more self-compassionate tend to be more in touch with their happiness, life satisfaction and motivation, and have better relationships and physical health. They also have the resilience needed to cope with stressful life events.

Quite often, compassionate people find it difficult to be compassionate towards themselves. And yet, it all starts there, within us, so start accepting yourself with gratitude, feeling grateful for who you are and the way you are, and loving yourself.

When we are mindful of our struggles, and respond to ourselves with compassion, kindness, and support in times of difficulty, things start to change. We can learn to embrace ourselves and our lives, despite inner and outer imperfections, and provide ourselves with the strength needed to really thrive.

*"If you want others to be happy, practice compassion.*
*If you want to be happy, practice compassion."*

*The Dalai Lama (1935- )*
*Spiritual leader and author*

# 12

## SLOWING DOWN

*I* have recently become aware that after the enforced "slowing down" of the pandemic lockdown, I have started to slip back into the maximum speed way of thinking and feeling, and it's just not enjoyable.

Life can often feel like it's zipping by in fast-forward. We feel obliged to accelerate our own speed along with it, until our productivity turns into frenzied accomplishment. We find ourselves cramming as much activity as possible into the shortest periods of time. We disregard our natural rhythms because it seems we have to just to keep up. In truth, rushing never gets you anywhere but on to the next activity or goal.

Slowing down allows you to not only savour your experiences, but also it allows you to fully focus your attention and energy on the task at hand. Moving at a slower place lets you get things done more efficiently, while rushing diminishes the quality of your work and your relationships. Slowing down also lets you be more mindful, deliberate, and fully present. When we slow down, we are giving ourselves the opportunity to reacquaint ourselves to our natural rhythms, and our inner wisdom. We let go of the "fast-forward" stress, and allow our bodies to remain centred and grounded.

Slowing down is inherent to fully savouring anything in life. Rushing to take a bath can feel like an uncomfortable dunk in hot water, while taking a slow, hot bubble bath can be luxuriant and relaxing. A student cramming for a test will often feel tired and unsure, whereas someone who really absorbs the information will be more confident and relaxed. Cooking, eating, reading, and writing can become pleasurable when done slowly. Slowing down lets you become more absorbed in whatever it is you are doing. The food you eat tastes better, and the stories you read become more alive.

Slowing down allows you to disconnect from the frenzied pace buzzing around you so you can begin moving at your own pace. The moments we choose to live in fast-forward motion then become a conscious choice rather than an involuntary action.

As we start to consistently slow down, we notice stillness. And in that stillness, we can contemplate our own mind. What we often find is that the mind is very restless. It wants to take care of a thousand things, because it's feeling some uncertainty and fear. It wants to fix problems, take care of all the undone things, and figure out if everything is going to be okay. It wants to get all of our needs met, from survival needs to meaning, connection and love.

What if we could allow our minds to rest?

We would need nothing in each moment, other than what's required for physical survival. That doesn't mean we do nothing (though we could!). There's calm and peace when we slow down. There's a feeling that we are enough. That everything we need is already contained within us.

Explore slowing down, find what works for you: it may be leaving more time to get to your destination, and then driving slower. It may be taking time to pause and breathe before you start the next task, or sitting down for five minutes and just being. It may be disconnecting your devices for a period of time; being online all the time means we're subject to interruptions and at the mercy of the demands of others. It's hard to slow down when you're always checking new messages coming in. Find what works for you.

Learning to slow down in our fast-moving world can take practice, it's a lifetime practice. When you slow down long enough to try it, you may surprise yourself with how fantastic living in this state can be.

# 13

## VALUE YOUR TIME

*S*o many of us feel a scarcity of time: we feel rushed, like there's not enough time to do everything, always behind, never feeling like we're doing enough. Most of us feel some kind of time stress: "I'm not making the most of my time, it's slipping away too fast, I'm overwhelmed by it all."

This problem is called "time scarcity," and it's one of the most common stresses in our society. So how do we deal with this? Unfortunately, there's no easy answer – but there are a few things I've found to be really helpful.

Firstly here are some things I have realised, and then I will show you some solutions to "time scarcity".

I realised: Nobody gets any more or less time than anyone else. We all get a fresh batch of twenty-four hours every day. Time is not a relevant variable for productivity. The variable is how much we try and fit into a unit of time. Generally speaking, we try to put too much into each chunk of time and therefore, we end up feeling overwhelmed. It's like we are trying to fit a gallon of "to-dos" into a pint glass! Personally, whenever I start to feel a little pressure or anxiety around time and my schedule, I know I have tried to fit too much in.

I realised: It doesn't matter how much you get done, doing more doesn't solve the problem of not enough time. I have had fantastically productive days, where I'll get twenty tasks done with no procrastination or distractions ... and I still feel like I need to do more, and that I wish I had more time.

I realised: That all we have is now, the present moment, and that in the present moment there is no past or future to consider. We all have as much "now" as there is to be had; when it comes to living now we already have all the time there is.

I realised: These hours really are precious. They are a gift. We take them for granted, and don't appreciate them to the fullest. We go through our days doing routine things, not really paying attention, and because of that ... the hours slip through our fingers, and we wonder where it all went.

So with these things in mind, I'll share some solutions that have helped me to make the most of my twenty-four hours most days.

First: Be intentional at the start of each day. I've found it important to take a few moments at the start of the day to reflect on what I want to do. I might not end up doing things exactly as I plan, but I'm much more likely to spend the hours wisely if I set intentions at the start. I make a list of what I would like for the day.

Second: Do what matters. Having a list of twenty things to do and doing twenty things in a day won't get rid of the time scarcity – in fact, it often makes the stress even worse. What if you had a list of three important things instead? If you could only put three things on the list, you'd choose carefully. As you do each of the three things on your list, do each thing to completion, and do each thing as if it were the only thing that mattered.

Third: Schedule "you time" every day. Within each of us, there is a well of energy that must be regularly replenished. When we act as if this well is bottomless, scheduling a long list of activities that fit like puzzle pieces into every minute of every day, it becomes depleted and we feel exhausted, disconnected, and weak. Refilling this well is a matter of finding time to focus on, nurture, and care for ourselves.

Fourth: Learn the skill of saying no. Practise saying no the right way. The three ingredients needed for a strong authentic "No" are: be logical; be polite; and be kind. Remember a request is an option, not an obligation.

Fifth: Reflect with gratitude. At the end of each day, take a few moments to reflect back on your day and think about things you're grateful for.

I've found this all helps to create an abundant state of mind around time.

Remember, I control what I do with my time. We all do, even when it seems out of control. Value your time. It is your life.

# 14

## LIVING ONE DAY AT A TIME

*Taking one step at a time makes life much easier to navigate, rather than always looking ahead.*

The years of our life do not arrive all at once; they greet us day by day. With the descent of each setting sun, we are able to rest our heads and let the world take care of itself for a while. We may rest assured throughout the night, knowing that the dawn will bring with it a chance to meet our lives anew, donning fresh perspectives and dream-inspired hopes. The hours that follow, before we return to sleep once more, are for us to decide how we want to live and learn, laugh and grow. Our lives are sweeter and more manageable when we experience them this way: one day at a time.

Imagine the future stretching out before you and try to notice if you feel any tension or overwhelm at the prospect of the journey still to come. Perhaps you have recently made a lifestyle change, like beginning a new diet or quitting smoking, and the idea of continuing this healthy new behaviour for years seems daunting. Maybe you have started a new business or are newly married and can feel an undercurrent of anxiety about your ability to succeed. Many years ago I can remember wanting to quit smoking in January but not doing so, because I was going to Las Vegas in October and I could not imagine being in Vegas with two other smokers and not smoking myself! When I did eventually quit, I did it by not having a cigarette one day at a time.

If you can shift your focus from what may happen years down the line and return it to the day that is before you right now, you may find a measure of calm and renewed confidence in your capabilities. You may also discover an inner faith that the future will take care of itself. The way we show up for our lives today and tomorrow has an enormous effect on who we will be and what we will be experiencing years from now. If we can remain fully engaged in the day at hand, enjoying all it has to offer and putting our energy into making the most of it, we will find that we are perfectly ready and capable to handle any future when it arrives.

# 15

## THERE IS ONLY NOW

*"People don't realize that now is all there ever is;
there is no past or future except as memory
or anticipation in your mind."*

*Eckhart Tolle (1948- )*
*German author and teacher*

*E*ven though everything that has ever happened to us up until this moment is in the dimension of thought, it is very real for us. While we can't touch or have any of it, we can certainly get quite emotional about it. It's crucial to understand this point. The whole experience of our past up until this very second is all in thought, and nothing more. How much sense does it make to be unhappy, to regret, or feel guilty about something that is just thought?

As for everything that's going to happen to us from this second on, understand that it is also nothing more than thought. We cannot eat tomorrow's breakfast today. We can't grab onto our goals. We can't take tomorrow's Mercedes and drive it. It's all thought. Yet we can also have the experience, within our form, through thought. If our whole past and our whole future are all thought, then all that leaves us with is now. So why would we choose to use up this moment with something like guilt or by continually thinking about things that have already happened. If feeling guilty doesn't do anything to correct what we are feeling guilty about, then stop doing it.

We hear people talking about "living in the past". But no one can live in the past, we can only live in the now. Similarly people say, "I worry because I live in the future." But they are not living in the future – they are using up this moment being consumed with future thinking over something that may or may not happen someday, over which they have no control. Waiting for "someday" is like striving for perfection, really just an excuse. "Someday" is a concept that exists only in the mind, not in reality.

It's such a sensible thing to get rid of that. You might ask how, and the answer is quite simple: You just do it.

There is only now, today, this present moment, this point in time. The only time that is, is now. The only thing we can do anything about is now. The past is gone, it's just stored thought, and some of that is not accurate. The future is just imagination, the future in the history of time has never ever showed up, yet we talk as though it's real. Just be in the now, now is always enough.

The way we show up for our lives today has an enormous effect on who we will be and what we will be experiencing years from now. If we can remain fully engaged in the now, enjoying all it has to offer and putting our energy into making the most of it, we will find that we are perfectly ready and capable to handle any future when it arrives.

Do not worry about your future. If we do our present well, our future will blossom.

# 16

## LIVING IN A RELAXED STATE

*E*ver since the first national lockdown, I have become a fan of slowing down, simplifying, doing less ... but what if you can't? What if your life can't be made less busy? Are you doomed to a life of anxiety, stress, and unhappiness? The answer is no! I'm going to share with you a very simple tool that might just transform your life. It's something I've been trying in the last few months, and I can attest that it works brilliantly.

This one little method will help you to:

- Be more present, so life doesn't rush past you without you noticing

- Enjoy every activity you do, so life is better all the time

- Feel more relaxed, so every day is as good as a holiday

- Be ready to handle anything that comes your way

Normally we have two different states in life. There's the busy state of our everyday lives, and then there's the relaxed state, which happens when we have some unstructured time: a holiday, a day at the beach, a spa break, time in the park with the kids. A relaxed state is one where we perhaps think less and feel more. We just soak in the sun, the sounds, and the sensations. This is a child-like state because it's the mode that young children are in the most. We do our best to train kids not to be like this, so they can be good workers when they grow up.

And so we grow up to be in the busy state most of the week, and if we're lucky we get a day or two at the weekend to be in a relaxed state. In reality it may be only an hour or two because the internet sucks us in, we have a less relaxed state because the internet keeps us in our minds, and we forget about the physical world around us.

How can we change this? How can we bring the child-like relaxed, sensory state back into our everyday lives, not just during breaks and meditation or yoga time and holidays? It's not that difficult if you practice.

## The Relaxed State

When we are in a relaxed state, we notice the sensations of the wind and sun, the sounds of water and laughter, the brilliant colours of nature, the smiles around us, the grass or sand between our toes. We are feeling instead of thinking. The sensations of our bodies flow into our minds relaxing us.

We can relearn this state of being with practice. Do it now. You're reading a computer or mobile device screen, so your mind is in the world of the internet ... but your body is in the physical world. If you're sitting, you can feel the chair. Your back might be a bit hunched, so straighten up. Your fingers are on a keyboard or mouse. Is the air around you cold or warm? Are there sounds you can notice? Is your jaw clenched? Notice your breathing.

When you put your focus on physical sensations, you are entering a relaxed state instead of thinking mode. It's not that you're completely relaxed, but you're in the same state of mind as the times you are relaxed, like yoga or at the beach or having a lie-in on a Sunday.

Once you learn to do this, you can do it anytime, anywhere. If you're taking a shower, feel the water running down you; soak in the temperature and the sound of running water. If you're eating, taste every little nuance of the food, smell the food, feel the texture in your mouth, and feel the movement of your hand going to your mouth.

Do this as you work [I am doing it as I write this, listening to the birds in my front and back garden], as you talk on the phone, respond to emails, walk to a meeting or drive to an appointment, noticing the sensations on your skin, the colours around you, the sounds of life, your breath coming in and leaving you. Do this at home, as you do chores, prepare food, clean up or get ready for work.

Do this throughout your day, and you will be in a constant state of relaxation and enjoyment. It will transform everything you do. It turns busy-ness into being present.

Life can be lived in a relaxed state.

# 17

## LET YOUR LIFE BE YOUR MESSAGE

*"You may have occasion to possess or use material things,
but the secret of life lies in never missing them."*

*Mahatma Gandhi (1869-1948)*
*Lawyer, political ethicist, writer, speaker*

Gandhi's life offers us many key lessons – he practiced simplicity and minimalism in all areas of his life and he left behind a huge legacy in how to live a life of simplicity. Gandhi was a man who died a pauper but who affected the lives of many, and continues to inspire us with his message even today. When Gandhi died, he had less than ten possessions, including a watch, spectacles, sandals and an eating bowl. He was a man of non-possession and didn't even own a house.

Gandhi was actually born into a prosperous family and had a very privileged upbringing, which included a prestigious education in England in the days when travel from India to England took many months by sea. He studied Law at University College, London and he was subsequently invited to join the Bar there. Though born into wealth, he ultimately gave it all away and through the course of his life, managed to let go of material trappings. He followed a life of simplicity.

Here are five great life lessons I learned from Gandhi, who was possibly the ultimate minimalist.

## 1. Accumulate little

Gandhi believed in possessing little except the clothes he wore and some utensils for cooking and eating. He used to give away or auction any gift that was ever given to him. It may not be possible these days for us to get down to less than ten possessions like he did, but start cutting down to bare basics. Recycle, give things away, or sell your unwanted possessions. I have lived many years now using the one-year strategy; if I have not worn something or used an item for over a year, I give it to charity. We tend to spend a lot of time and energy looking after our possessions. By having fewer things to possess and look after, your life naturally becomes simpler.

## 2. Eat simple food

Gandhi never had a problem with being overweight. He followed a strict vegetarian diet and drank mostly water, frequently cooking his own simple food, which was locally produced. He ate this simple food from a small bowl, a reminder to eat moderately, and at the same time he ate mindfully, often accompanied by prayers. So eat simply and moderately.

He said, *"Experience has taught me that it was wrong to have dwelt upon the relish of food. One should eat not in order to please the palate, but to keep the body going."*

## 3. Dress simply

Gandhi wore simple clothes that conveyed his message. There is this anecdotal story of when Gandhi met King George V of the United Kingdom in London and he wore his simple wrap-around cloth. A journalist asked Gandhi, "Mr Gandhi, did you feel underdressed when you met the King?" Gandhi replied, "The King was wearing enough clothes for both of us!"

Simplify your life by dressing for comfort, not to impress.

## 4. Lead a simple, stress-free life

Gandhi never got stressed. He meditated daily and spent hours in reflection and prayer. Though he was a world leader and idolised by millions, he continued to lead a simple life with few distractions and commitments. He would even interrupt his political meetings to go off and play with children. And despite all his needs being taken care of, Gandhi still insisted on doing his own simple things. He advocated self-sufficiency and simple work.

So don't take life too seriously – remember to take time out to play.

## 5. Let your life be your message

Though he was a prolific writer and powerful speaker, in private Gandhi spoke very quietly and only when necessary. He was also very punchy and concise in his writing. He preferred to let his life do the talking for him. By living a simple life, Gandhi was able to devote his life to his chosen higher purpose.

He was totally focused on his commitment to his people and the world. Even if you don't wish to be another Gandhi, your life will be much simpler and happier by following some or all of these life lessons. As he said, *"You must be the change you wish to see in the world."*

Start living a simpler life from today – and you will release a lot of time and energy. This will give you the space to create the life you really want to live, a life that is inspired and inspiring.

Ask yourself; does what you do and how you live, convey your message to the world?

*"Live simply so that others may simply live."*

*Mahatma Gandhi (1869-1948)*
*Lawyer, political ethicist, writer, speaker*

# 18

## THINKING ABOUT IT OR DOING IT

*I* spend a lot of time dreaming about things – incredible adventures I want to go on, countries I wish to visit, self-improvement retreats and projects, and all those books I plan on reading and listening to! And there's nothing wrong with that. Dreaming is wonderful. What I've noticed, though, is that sometimes I get stuck in the thinking and dreaming mode, and don't actually take action.

I dream about going on these epic walks or bike rides through the mountains ... I research it, learn about it, plan out my gear and routes ... but I'm stuck inside, doing all of this research and planning. I'm not actually outside, experiencing the walk or the bike ride. When I realise this, it's good for me to make this distinction: am I in the mode of thinking about it, or actually doing it? Both are fine! But at some point, it helps to make the switch: from thinking about it ... to doing it.

This is the point where we make a commitment. We go from considering whether to take the plunge with a big decision … to committing ourselves to a course of action. Taking action is like leaping off a cliff; there's no looking back!

What areas in your life are you thinking about? What kind of commitment would it take to put you into doing mode? And how much longer would you like to wait? You'll seldom experience regret for anything that you've done. It is what you haven't done that will torment you.

Are you here to experience life or to think about it? Many people overthink everything, whether to call an old friend, whether to go out at the weekend, and whether to take up that new class. Overthinking takes you away from the heart and keeps you frozen inside the thinking mind. Don't think, just do.

The message, therefore, is clear. Do it!

One day you will wake up and there won't be any more time to do the things you've always wanted. So do it now.

# 19

## FINDING JOY IN DOING

*W*henever we're trying to learn something, get better at anything, or change something ... we have a certain hope or idea of how we'll make progress. We imagine starting to run or work out, starting to lose those extra pounds, and in a mere couple of weeks, we should be doing as well as the people we see on YouTube or in books and magazines. We should very quickly drop weight, never ever look at a doughnut again, and be perfect in everything we do.

Of course, that sounds crazy when I write it out like that, but in reality, we all have hopes that are similarly unrealistic. We hope to learn something instantly, to quickly be good at whatever we're trying to master, and hit our goals with incredible accuracy. Our efforts never live up to these hopes. And it discourages us, makes us think we're doing something wrong, often causing us to stop trying, to say, "Forget it!"

My message is to encourage you to forget about those hopes, ideals and expectations of progress. They're never, ever realistic. Never. Instead, can you find joy in the doing? Can you find joy in every run, every workout, and every learning session? Can you be fully present, as much as possible, and let go of any image you have in your head of the future? Well, even if you can't – keep going!

A friend recently shared this story with me by the American writer, Kurt Vonnegut, and it is a total game changer. It takes away any discouragement and is wisdom I wish I had heard at an early age.

> When I was 15, I spent a month working on an archaeological dig. I was talking to one of the archaeologists one day during our lunch break and he asked those kinds of "getting to know you" questions you ask young people: Do you play sports? What's your favourite subject? And I told him, *"No, I don't play any sports. I do theatre, I'm in the choir, I play the violin and piano, and I used to take art classes."*
>
> And he said, *"WOW. That's amazing!"* And I said, *"Oh no, but I'm not any good at any of them."* And he said something then that I will never forget and which absolutely blew my mind because no one had ever said anything like it to me before.
>
> He said, *"I don't think being good at things is the point of doing them. I think you've got all these wonderful experiences with different skills and that all teaches you*

*things and make you an interesting person, no matter how well you do them."*

And that honestly changed my life. Because I went from a failure, someone who hadn't been talented enough at anything to excel, to someone who did things because I enjoyed them. I had been raised in such an achievement-oriented environment, so inundated with the myth of 'Talent', that I thought it was only worth doing things if you could 'Win' at them.

Isn't that incredible? This story both inspired and changed me. As an example, I now write just for the joy of it. Try this with anything and everything. What I have found is that it totally changes your state and expectation around any life experience.

# 20

## GOING THE EXTRA MILE

An Indian farmer had become old and ready to pass his farm down to one of his two sons. When he brought his sons together to speak about it, he told them, "I intend for the farm to go to the younger son."

The older son was furious! "What are you talking about? That's not fair!" he fumed.

The father sat patiently, thinking.

"Okay," the father said, "I need you both to do something for me. We need more cows. Will you go to Ramesh's farm and see if he has any cows for sale?"

The older son shortly returned and reported, "Father, Ramesh has six cows for sale."

The father graciously thanked the older son for his work. He then turned to the younger son and said, " We need more cows. Will you go to Ramesh's farm and see if he has any cows for sale?"

The younger son did as he was asked. A short while later, he returned and reported, "Father, Ramesh has six cows for sale. Each cow will cost 2,000 rupees. If we are thinking about buying all six cows, Ramesh said he would be willing to reduce the price by one hundred rupees per cow. Ramesh also said they are getting special Jersey cows next week so if we aren't in a hurry, it may be good to wait. However, if we need the cows urgently, Ramesh said he could deliver the cows tomorrow."

The father graciously thanked the younger son for his work. He then turned to the older son and said, "That's why I am passing the farm onto your younger brother."

For the most part, most people are like the older son in the story. Most people could be easily replaced. Most people are passive and reactive. They require specific instructions. They need to be managed in most things.

Conversely, those who become successful are fully engaged in a good cause. They don't need to be managed in all things. They don't just do the job, they do it right and complete it. Most importantly, those who become successful go the extra mile. They reach out to people, ask questions, make recommendations, offer to help, and pitch their ideas. Being successful requires being proactive and not waiting for life to come to you. It means you're active, not passive.

Going the extra mile always involves some degree of risk. You're putting yourself out there and there is a chance you could fail. Conversely, doing only what you're told entails no risk and carries no responsibility. It's playing safe.

I have found that if you can be the most enthusiastic person you know, then you won't go far wrong. Enthusiasm so often makes the critical difference: it keeps you going when times are tough, it encourages everyone around you, it allows you to go the extra mile and it soon becomes a habit.

Being prepared to do whatever it takes and to go the extra mile is the one behaviour that separates the successful from the average in life.

# 21

## GET INSPIRED

*"You owe it to us all to get on with what you're good at."*

*W. H. Auden (1907-1973)*
*British-American poet*

Yesterday as I walked among the mass of humanity in the centre of Reading town, two men with microphones and a "Trust Jesus" sign started singing the good word to the crowd.

They were ignored, of course, but what caught my attention was that they both had a radiant smile, and I couldn't help but notice their energy and enthusiasm. Say what you want about them (possibly a little crazy?), but they were both so much more excited about something than any of the lunchtime workers and shoppers who went out of their way to avoid them.

They were inspired and moved to get up on a soapbox and do something!

How many of us can claim to be that excited about anything we do? If you don't get excited by what you do, ask yourself, why not? I can honestly say I am excited by what I do. Not to the point where I'm screaming about it on a street corner, but excited nonetheless. What most people are missing is inspiration, and the conviction that they are doing something good, that might change the lives of others.

We all have days when we're just not very inspired, when we need passion and creativity breathed into us. I know I do. For anyone who needs a little shove, whose creativity has dried up, who needs to be moved … I humbly offer this simple guide. While I never claim to have all the answers, nor that my way is the only way, I share here some things I've learned about inspiration, some tricks I've learned that work for me.

I'm often in need of inspiration, and in all cases, I've found it. And it's a wonderful thing.

## What is Inspiration?

Many people think of it as an elusive quality that can't be forced, and yet it can be found if you look for it. Others think it's a way to find ideas, but it's more than ideas … it's being moved to put those ideas into action…

## How to Find Inspiration

Inspiration is just about everywhere you can look, if you're looking for it. That's the key: to keep your eyes open. Too often we miss beautiful sources of inspiration, because we're too busy thinking about other things. Be curious. See everything around you as a possible source of inspiration.

Some possible sources of inspiration:

- Blogs
- Books
- Magazines
- Films
- The people around you
- Nature
- Children
- Art
- Music
- Exercise
- Religion
- Dreams
- Social media
- Photographs
- The Internet
- Success stories

Just keep your eyes open at all times, staying present whenever possible, and allow yourself to attract that inspiration.

## How to Stay Inspired

Inspiration isn't just a one-time thing. You'll need it on a regular basis. When you practice the above method – keeping your eyes open, staying present, being aware of inspiration – you get better at it.

Here are some tips for keeping the inspiration coming:

- Surround yourself with inspired people – one of the best ways to stay inspired is to be with creative, energetic, positive people.

- Read and listen daily – varied things, from blogs to magazines, to podcasts of all kinds.

- Get outside – nature is one of my biggest inspirations, and you'll miss it if you're inside all day.

- Talk with new people – they'll always expose you to new and interesting things, if you're open to it.

- Break out of your routine – see things from a different perspective. Take a new route home. Go to a new restaurant. Visit a new area in your town.

- Find time for silence – it's more inspiring than you might think.

- Exercise – or at least get moving. It helps the blood to circulate, and get ideas moving around. A lot of my inspired thoughts come during walks.

- Travel – I always return from foreign travel with new ideas and inspiration. As an example, I felt inspired watching the sunrise on Machu Picchu, and I also found inspiration on a golf trip to Portugal. For me, it could come on any trip.

Find Inspiration. Find something that moves you. Get inspired.

**Now Take Action.** Don't just feel inspired. Take this inspiration and use it, be moved, and do something. Channel that inspiration into creating something amazing. Put that something out into the world, and in turn, you will inspire others.

Go out and do something good. I promise you, it will change your life.

# 22

## THE TRAGEDY AND LIBERATION OF DEATH

*R*ecently, one of my closest school friends told me he had been given the tragic news that he had possibly twelve months left to live. Two days later I heard the tragic news of a lovely golfing friend passing away at what I consider to be an early age. I'm still in shock, and coming to terms with both bits of news. My heart goes out to all the family members of both my friends.

And of course, it makes me appreciate the loved ones I do have. I've been thinking of all of them, grateful that I've had so many good moments with all of them. This sudden news has made me face my own mortality this week. I know it is coming, just not when. I rarely think about it, because life is so in-my-face, but it's there, waiting. A friend's death is such a stark reminder that we never know how much time we have left.

I've been contemplating this quote from a revered Zen teacher and writer, Joan Halifax.

*"From the perspective of many wisdom traditions, death is seen as the ultimate moment for the complete liberation of the mind from all entanglements, all sorrows and all separateness."*

And there is something liberating about this for me. When I die, I will no longer imagine myself as separate from the world. I will no longer imagine that I'm somehow not good enough, nor worry about all the fears that come from that idea of inadequacy. At the moment of death, I will suddenly no longer try to control others, or burden myself with my judgements of others.

This is indisputable. And if it's true … why can't I just let go of those things right now? Why waste time with trying to control or judge others, with worrying about whether I'm good enough, with insisting on my separation from everything else? It all takes so much energy. Why not just free myself of these things today, instead of waiting for the moment of death? The gift of deciding to face your mortality, is the gift of recognising that because you will die, you must live now.

# 23

## THE COMFORT IN NOT KNOWING

### The Parable of the Chinese Farmer

A farmer and his son had a beloved stallion that helped the family earn a living. One day, the horse ran away and their neighbours exclaimed, "Your horse ran away, what terrible luck!"

The farmer replied, "Maybe so, maybe not. We'll see."

A few days later, the horse returned home, leading a few wild mares back to the farm as well. The neighbours shouted out, "Your horse has returned, and brought several horses home with him. What great luck!"

The farmer replied, "Maybe so, maybe not. We'll see."

Later that week, the farmer's son was trying to break one of the mares and she threw him to the ground, breaking his leg. The villagers cried, "Your son broke his leg, what terrible luck!"

The farmer replied, "Maybe so, maybe not. We'll see."

A few weeks later, soldiers from the national army marched through town, recruiting all the able-bodied boys for the army. They did not take the farmer's son, still recovering from his broken leg. Friends shouted, "Your boy is spared, what tremendous luck!"

To which the farmer replied, "Maybe so, maybe not. We'll see."

The moral of this story provides a powerful lesson. The truth is, we don't know what's going to happen, we just **think** we do. No event, in and of itself, can truly be judged as good or bad, lucky or unlucky, fortunate or unfortunate, as only time will tell the whole story. Additionally, no one really lives long enough to find out the 'whole story,' so it could be considered a great waste of time to judge minor inconveniences as misfortunes, or to invest tons of energy into things that look outstanding on the surface, but may not pay off in the end.

The wiser thing, then, is to live life taking all things in our stride, whether they originally appear to be 'good' or 'bad.' Life is much more comfortable and comforting if we merely accept what we're given and make the best of our life circumstances. Rather than always having to pass judgement on things and declare them as good or bad, maybe it would be better to remember, "Maybe so, maybe not. We'll see."

# 24

## FREEDOM THROUGH DECLUTTERING

 $\mathcal{W}$ e're living in a time when many of us feel overloaded with stress. Yet many of us don't realise how our personal habits may be contributing to our anxiety and distress. Clutter can affect our anxiety levels, our sleep, and ability to focus. After all, decluttering not only makes it easier to find what you're looking for by creating space in your home, it can also create space in your mind.

When we go through the process of decluttering, we feel a sense of freedom and control. Decluttering our home or workspace can often seem overwhelming, but in truth, it can be a way to practice living mindfully and in the moment.

Here's why.

1. Clutter is a manifestation of holding onto the past and a fear of what might happen in the future.

2. Letting go of clutter is a way to live more mindfully and in the present.

3. The act of decluttering itself can be a mindfulness practice.

Let's talk about each of those things briefly.

Clutter is holding onto the past, for fear of the future.

Why do we have clutter in the first place? Why do we keep it when we don't really need it? Maybe we think we do need it, for two reasons:

1. We don't want to let go of the past. Often, clutter comes in the form of emotional attachment to objects that have significance to us. They might remind us of a loved one, or a vacation, or a special event like a birthday, funeral, graduation and so on. It might be a gift from someone. All of this is living in the past. I'm not saying we should forget about the past, but letting go of these objects (and they're only objects, they're not the events or loved ones themselves), is a way of releasing our hold on the past. It's a way of living more in the present. I never forget the past, but it's not a place I try to dwell.

2. We're afraid of the future. Clutter might be things we think we might need sometime in the future. We hold on to them, just in case. Overpacking for a trip is a good

example – we bring more clothes than we really need, just in case we need them. It's the same in our houses – we have many things we don't really need or use, just in case. We're afraid of being unprepared for the future, but the truth is we can never be totally prepared. We can't control the outcome of the future, and trying to do so means that we're never really living in the present moment. We're always preparing for what might (or might not) come.

Look at your clutter carefully, one object at a time, and ask yourself why you're holding onto each object. If you're honest, it's probably for one of these two reasons.

Books are a great example. We hold onto books we've already read, as trophies of our reading accomplishments, and we hold onto books thinking we might read them again in the future. In truth, you only need three or four books – the ones you might read in the next month. Then after you've read those, give them away or donate those books to charity.

Let go of clutter to live mindfully.

So if clutter is holding onto the past, and fearing the future … how can we live in the present instead?

As we get rid of clutter, we release our mind of these attachments and fears. It's a liberating process. Clutter is the physical embodiment of these attachments and fears – emotional stuff that we don't realise we have. By decluttering, we are clearing ourselves of these tangled webs. And when we've got rid of clutter, we are free. We can forget about those things, and live instead in this moment. We can fully appreciate life as it happens, instead of looking back on what has happened before, or looking forward to what might happen later.

It is of course possible to live in the moment even if you have clutter. But decluttering can be a beautiful process of helping ourselves let go of the things we don't realise we're holding on to. And so, as I declutter, not only am I freeing myself up to live in the present ... I am living in the present during the process of decluttering.

And decluttering is one of the best mindfulness practices, in my experience. Here's how I do it, using a desk drawer as an example:

1. Don't worry about all the rest of your cluttered spaces for now – just pick one space. Small is good.

2. Empty the drawer. Take everything out, putting it in a pile somewhere. Clean the drawer while it's clear.

3. Take one object from the pile. Forget about the entire pile – just look at that one object. Ask yourself why you have it. Is it for emotional reasons, or do you really use it? Is it for "just in case"? When was the last time you used it? If you don't really need or use it, put it in a box for donation or bin it. If you do really use it, put it in another pile to be put back in your now-clean drawer. If you're on the fence and can't bear to give something up, put it in a 'maybe' box and put that box away for six months.

4. Repeat, one object at a time. Practice doing this mindfully. Make a decision with each object – keep, donate, or 'maybe' box. No waffling or putting off decisions. Learn to focus on one thing at a time, mindfully, and deal with each object only once. This is a good practice for doing anything.

5. And here is a great tip from Pamela Hatswell who reached out to me after reading this blog. "There is one more powerful way of approaching the decluttering issue especially as you get older. If it's not you but someone else, perhaps a member of your family, that will next look at the embarrassing contents of the drawer/loft/garage, will they understand why that object is there? So if there is a story, a name, or a value then write it down or put a label on it. Helping the next generation understand the things we do keep is worthwhile, and it also helps us clear things we know they don't need, want, or would be able to make sense of."

The decluttering process creates both physical space and calendar space, and as a result, creates mental space, all of which give us a sense of freedom.

# 25

## OVERCOMING OVERWHELM

*F*eeling overwhelmed with work and personal tasks is one of the biggest problems that people are facing in today's busy world. It feels like there's so much to do, never enough time to do it, and who knows what we should focus on? We're always behind, barely treading water. That's our usual experience of life. When there's a pile of undone things, it can feel pretty overwhelming – how in the world can we tackle all of that? It can be stressful and shut us down to actually doing anything at all.

There are two practices that have helped me:

1.  One task at a time until finished

2.  Find delight in the task

## One Task at a Time until Finished

First, I make a list of things I need to do. Making a simple list like this can really help get everything out in plain sight and let you see what you're up against. This is where people often feel overwhelmed, so if you start to get stuck here, just move to the next part.

Second, I make a short priority list of what I want to focus on for today. I can't do the whole list today, so I chop it down to what I would love to accomplish just for today. I try to keep this list short so I don't get too overwhelmed and it feels doable. If it doesn't feel doable, I make it shorter!

Finally, I pick one task and really focus on that until it's finished. Normally I pick a small one, something doable that I can use to get some momentum. Then that task becomes my whole world. When my mind starts to go to all the other things on the list ... I simply return to that one task and give it all my full focus. Sometimes I can still feel a little overwhelmed because I still have a big list left. The way I think about it is firstly, I am doing the best I can and secondly, I am doing the most important things first.

## Find Delight in the Task

Okay, so we do one task at a time ... the challenge is that it can still often feel like we're just trying to get through the list, rushing through tasks, not really loving what we're doing. What if you could find delight in the tasks? What if it could be an adventure, or a way of expressing your love for others?

As I take each task off the list and give it my full focus, I try to find a reason why I care about this. I find a reason to be excited by it, a reason to enjoy what I'm doing. I get fired up about the task, and put my full self into it. I find the adventure in the task. Every task has this possibility in it. We just need to find it.

What could excite you about your tasks today?

# 26

## LIFELONG LEARNING

*"We cannot become what we want by remaining what we are."*

*Max De Pree (1924-2017)*
*American businessman and writer*

*I*n today's distracted world, most people spend more time being mindlessly entertained than they do developing their skills and learning their craft. So what are you doing right now to further your education in what you're passionate about? Are you waiting for the right opportunity to come knocking before you develop the skills you need for it?

Get ready now! Fascination is the key to learning, get curious about your topic. If you can't get fascinated, you won't care enough to really learn something. The more information you have, the more prepared you will be when opportunity knocks. I pour myself into it. I will read or listen to every book I can get my hands on.

Reading for just an hour a day will greatly increase both your knowledge and your level of success. There are so many things to read and listen to, from finance to psychology, from economics to business, from health to computers. For one hour a day, you could be studying a wide array of subjects that could help you live a better life.

Successful people didn't wait for someone to call on them to be an expert before they gathered all the knowledge they could about their subject. They were ready when the opportunities presented themselves. Spend your time reading and learning, read biographies and autobiographies to study the ways of other successful people. Read often, review what you've read, and apply at least one thing that you've learned.

Attend anything that may help: conferences, trade shows, training seminars. Remember to be teachable! You can't learn a thing if you think you already know it all. Listen to those who have achieved success in your field. Open up to letting others point you in the right direction. After all, you can always try something out and if it doesn't work for you, you can discard it.

And as you start to succeed, don't stop your learning habits. Keep up with your industry. Keep making improvements. Keep studying the masters. Become powerful by being as knowledgeable as you can be, by learning new ways to do things, and by being more effective and efficient in your life. The books you lose yourself in can lead you on paths of discovery that take you out of your own life and help you see that existence can unfold in an infinite number of ways. You can learn so much from the characters and mentors who guide you from page to page.

Continuous learning has played a major part in all aspects of my life. And I am so proud to see that my three children have all adopted this wonderful habit in their own lives and careers.

# 27

## DO WHAT YOU LOVE

*I* love these three powerful messages adapted from Steve Jobs' 2005 University of Stanford Commencement talk. I feel they all point to a better way to live.

### Connecting the Dots

I dropped out of Reed College after six months, but then stayed around as a drop-in for another eighteen months or so before I really quit. So why did I drop out?

It started before I was born. My biological mother was a young, un-wed college graduate student, and she decided to put me up for adoption. She felt very strongly that I should be adopted by college graduates, so everything was all set for me to be adopted at birth by a lawyer and his wife. Except that when I popped out they decided at the last minute that they really wanted a girl. So my parents, who were on a waiting list, got a call in the middle of the night asking, "We have an unexpected baby boy; do you want him?" They said, "Of course!" My biological mother later found out that my mother had never graduated from college and that my father had never graduated from high school. She refused to sign the final adoption papers. She only relented a few months later when my parents promised that I would someday go to college.

And seventeen years later I did go to college. But I naively chose a college that was almost as expensive as Stanford, and all of my working-class parents' savings were being spent on my college tuition. After six months, I couldn't see the value in it. I had no idea what I wanted to do with my life and no idea how college was going to help me figure it out. And here I was spending all of the money my parents had saved their entire life. So I decided to drop out and trust that it would all work out OK. It was pretty scary at the time, but looking back it was one of the best decisions I ever made. The minute I dropped out I could stop taking the required classes that didn't interest me, and begin dropping in on the ones that looked interesting.

It wasn't all romantic. I didn't have a dorm room, so I slept on the floor in friends' rooms, I returned Coke bottles for the five cents deposits to buy food with, and I would walk the seven miles across town every Sunday night to get one good meal a week at the Hare Krishna temple. I loved it. And much of what I stumbled into by following my curiosity and intuition turned out to be priceless later on. Let me give you one example:

Reed College at that time offered perhaps the best calligraphy instruction in the country. Throughout the campus every poster, every label on every drawer, was beautifully hand calligraphed. Because I had dropped out and didn't have to take the normal classes, I decided to take a calligraphy class to learn how to do this. I learned about serif and sans serif typefaces, about varying the amount of space between different letter combinations, about what makes great typography great. It was beautiful, historical, artistically subtle in a way that science can't capture, and I found it fascinating.

None of this had even a hope of any practical application in my life. But ten years later, when we were designing the first Macintosh computer, it all came back to me. And we designed it all into the Mac. It was the first computer with beautiful typography. If I had never dropped in on that single course in college, the Mac would have never had multiple typefaces or proportionally spaced fonts. And since Windows just copied the Mac, it's likely that no personal computer would have them. If I had never dropped out, I would have never dropped in on this calligraphy class, and personal computers might not have the wonderful typography that they do. Of course it was impossible to connect the dots looking forward when I was in college. But it was very, very clear looking backward ten years later.

Again, you can't connect the dots looking forward; you can only connect them looking backward. So you have to trust that the dots will somehow connect in your future. You have to trust in something — your gut, the universe, life, karma, whatever. This approach has never let me down, and it has made all the difference in my life.

## Love and Loss

I was lucky – I found what I loved to do early in life. Woz and I started Apple in my parents' garage when I was twenty. We worked hard, and in ten years Apple had grown from just the two of us in a garage into a two-billion-dollar company with over 4,000 employees. We had just released our finest creation, the Macintosh, a year earlier, and I had just turned thirty. And then I got fired.

How can you get fired from a company you started? Well, as Apple grew we hired someone who I thought was very talented to run the company with me, and for the first year or so things went well. But then our visions of the future began to diverge and eventually we had a falling out. When we did, our Board of Directors sided with him. So at 30 I was out. And very publicly out. What had been the focus of my entire adult life was gone, and it was devastating.

I really didn't know what to do for a few months. But something slowly began to dawn on me – I still loved what I did. The turn of events at Apple had not changed that one bit. I had been rejected, but I was still in love. And so I decided to start over. I didn't see it then, but it turned out that getting fired from Apple was the best thing that could have ever happened to me. The heaviness of being successful was replaced by the lightness of being a beginner again, less sure about everything. It freed me to enter one of the most creative periods of my life.

During the next five years, I started a company named NeXT, another company named Pixar, and fell in love with an amazing woman who would become my wife. Pixar went on to create the world's first computer animated feature film, *Toy Story*, and is now the most successful animation studio in the world. In a remarkable turn of events, Apple bought NeXT, I returned to Apple, and the technology we developed at NeXT is at the heart of Apple's current renaissance. And Laurene and I have a wonderful family together.

I'm pretty sure none of this would have happened if I hadn't been fired from Apple. Sometimes life hits you in the head with a brick. Don't lose faith. I'm convinced that the only thing that kept me going was that I loved what I did. You've got to find what you love. And that is as true for your work as it is for your lovers. Your work is going to fill a large part of your life, and the only way to be truly satisfied is to do what you believe is great work. And the only way to do great work is to love what you do. If you haven't found it yet, keep looking. Don't settle. As with all matters of the heart, you'll know when you find it. And, like any great relationship, it just gets better and better as the years roll on. So keep looking until you find it. Don't settle.

## Death

When I was seventeen, I read a quote that went something like, "If you live each day as if it was your last, someday you'll most certainly be right." It made an impression on me, and since then, for the past thirty-three years, I have looked in the mirror every morning and asked myself: "If today were the last day of my life, would I want to do what I am about to do today?" And whenever the answer has been "No" for too many days in a row, I know I need to change something.

Remembering that I'll be dead soon is the most important tool I've ever encountered to help me make the big choices in life. Because almost everything – all external expectations, all pride, all fear of embarrassment or failure – these things just fall away in the face of death, leaving only what is truly important. Remembering that you are going to die is the best way I know to avoid the trap of thinking you have something to lose. You are already naked. There is no reason not to follow your heart.

No one wants to die. Even people who want to go to heaven don't want to die to get there. And yet death is the destination we all share. No one has ever escaped it. And that is as it should be, because Death is very likely the single best invention of Life. It is Life's change agent. It clears out the old to make way for the new. Right now the new is you, but someday not too long from now, you will gradually become the old and be cleared away. Sorry to be so dramatic, but it is quite true.

Your time is limited, so don't waste it living someone else's life. Don't let the noise of others' opinions drown out your own inner voice.

And most important; have the courage to follow your heart and intuition. They somehow already know what you truly want to become. Everything else is secondary.

# 28

## AWARENESS

$\mathcal{L}$ife is a journey comprised of many steps on our personal path that take us down a winding road of constant evolution. Each day, we are provided with a host of opportunities that can allow us to transform. One moment we can be presented with an opportunity to react differently when someone in our life rubs us up the wrong way; on another day, we may find ourselves wanting to change a particular habit but are not sure if we can. Eventually, we may find ourselves stuck in a rut that we can never seem to get out of.

It is during these moments that awareness can be the first step to change. Awareness is when we are able to realise what we are doing. We observe ourselves, noticing our reactions, actions, and choices as if we were watching a film. Awareness is the first step to change, because we can't make a change unless we are aware that one needs to be made in the first place. We can then begin to understand why we are doing what we are doing. Afterwards, it becomes difficult not to change because we are no longer asleep to the truth behind our behaviours. We also begin to realise that, just as much as we are the root source behind the causes for our behaviours, we are also the originator for any changes that we want to happen.

Here is an awareness example from my own experience. I recently started a new role as a volunteer with a charity and was going through the training with a group of ten others. At the start of the training I was excited and full of both joy and anticipation regarding the role. As we approached the end of the program we started to role play and were paired up with another new volunteer. I was paired with a lovely lady and we did two sessions together, lasting about thirty minutes each. By the end of the second session I had compared myself with her and decided that I was not good enough. I felt like an imposter and my initial excitement and joy had vanished.

Luckily, within a week I had read the quote, "Comparison is the thief of all joy" by Theodore Roosevelt. It helped me to create a new awareness around the whole experience.

What is it about comparison which robs us of joy?

Comparing ourselves with others is fairly universal. Comparison itself is not what robs us of our joy. The issue is to whom we are comparing ourselves to and why? Comparison to those we think are succeeding, particularly when we believe we are not, can become a toxic thought problem. It comes down to the narrative that we are playing out in our minds. Comparison cuts in when we believe someone else can do what we are doing better than us. Fear and imposter syndrome can take over and before we know where we are, it has undermined our confidence, we feel rubbish about ourselves, and we have lost our joy.

However, we can use comparison to our advantage, but it requires us to change the message. When the thought enters our mind, "I am not good enough", or "They are much better at this than I am," then switch the narrative.

In my example I needed to look back and see how far I had come. Possibly I was not as good a listener as the lovely lady I was partnered with at that point. But was I making progress? Was I a better listener than I was last year? Was I learning from what I was doing? I needed to admit that I was a 'work in progress'. I needed to acknowledge that I was getting better, more professional, upgrading my knowledge and understanding. When I changed my narrative, I realised I was heading in the right direction and that the results would take care of themselves.

If you suffer from this problem, it is important to change your thoughts and mindset before you find yourself heading down this unhelpful rabbit hole and being robbed of your joy.

There is a freedom that comes with awareness. Rather than thinking that we are stuck in a repetitive cycle where there is no escape, we begin to see that we very much play a hand in creating our lives. Whether we are aware of them or not, our behaviours and choices are always ours to make. Our past no longer has to dictate our future when we choose to be aware. We are then free to move beyond our old limits, make new choices, and take new actions. With awareness, our paths can't help but wind us forward in our lives while paving the way for new experiences and new ways of being. It is through awareness that we continue to consciously evolve.

*"I am not what happened to me ,*
*I am what I choose to become."*

*Carl Jung (1875-1961)*
*Swiss psychiatrist and psychoanalyst*

# 29

## THE POWER OF 'NO'

*J*was nearly forty years old before I started to learn to say No. Saying No to somebody when we're used to saying Yes can be challenging, as most of us fear being rejected.

From early childhood, many of us are taught that saying Yes is right and saying No is wrong. We learn that giving in to demands allows us to avoid conflict and criticism, to please people, earn praise, and prove that we care for the important people in our lives. Yet the right to say No is indelibly intertwined with our ability to make choices. When we sense we are limited in our options, compelled to say Yes even when doing so is not in our interests, we are effectively robbed of our ability to choose. Growing out of this tendency to say Yes even when we desperately want to say No can be challenging, because we suspect that others will reject us for our assertiveness. But the reward we receive upon facing this challenge is true freedom of choice.

When others ask you to take on work or do favours, consider their requests carefully. If you feel pressed to say Yes, consider whether you are accepting something reluctantly out of a desire for approval or to avoid disapproval. Remind yourself often that the ability to say No is an important aspect of well-being, as it is an indication that you understand the true value of your energy, talents, and time.

As you learn to say No, be aware that you may initially get out of balance by saying it too often. The word NO may even become your default response for some time. When you see that life moves forward without interruption, however, you will grow more comfortable saying No and will resume making decisions from a point of balance.

It took me a long time to realise that I was a people-pleaser, and the majority of my efforts went into pleasing others and making them happy. Yet quite often, despite my best efforts, I found that people did not always appreciate what I had done, and it would leave me feeling disheartened and upset. Everything changed for me when a mentor shared a totally different way of looking at this scenario. He taught me that whatever I do is for myself. And when I recognise this fact, I will never do anything just to please others. When I am content with the effort I put in, I will never be dependent on others' recognition of what I have done. When I enjoy everything I do, I will be truly content.

Remember, when you say Yes to one thing, you are saying No to something else. However, there is nothing inherently wrong with agreeing to requests others make of you, provided these requests do not infringe upon your peace of mind. Keep in mind that it is only when you feel you have the right to say No that you can say Yes with certainty, sincerity and enthusiasm. While saying Yes almost always has a price, you can feel good about offering your agreement when your reasons for doing so are rooted in your individual values, and your appreciation for the appeal before you.

# 30

## QUITTING THE WORRY HABIT

*W*orry is an extension of fear, and can also set you up for attracting that which you don't want in your life.

We have all had the experience of worrying about something at some point in our lives. Some of us have a habitual tendency to worry, and all of us have known someone who is a chronic worrier. Worry can be a very draining experience. In order for worry to exist, we have to imagine that something bad might happen. However, what we are worrying about has not happened yet, so this bad thing is by definition, a fantasy. Understood this way, worry is a self-created state of needless fear. Think of all the times you have worried over something that never ever happened.

One reason we worry is because we feel like we're not in control. For example, you might worry about your loved ones driving home in bad weather. There is nothing you can do to guarantee their safe journey, but you worry until you find out they have reached their destination unharmed. In this instance, worry is an attempt to feel useful and in control. However, worrying does nothing to ensure a positive outcome and it has an unpleasant effect on your body, mind, and spirit.

The good news is that there are ways to transform this kind of worry so that it has a healing effect. Just as worry uses the imagination, so does the antidote to worry. Next time you find that you are worrying, imagine the best result instead of anticipating the worst outcome. Visualise your loved ones and clearly see in your mind's eye their safe arrival home. Generate peace and well-being instead of nervousness and unease within yourself.

Another reason we worry is when we put something off – an unpaid parking ticket, revising for an upcoming test, dealing with an issue with a friend. In these cases, acknowledging that we are worried and taking action is the best solution. If you can confront the situation and take responsibility to change it, you'll have no reason to worry.

Dr Wayne Dyer helped me personally to understand a solution to worry. He says, "If something is out of my control then there is no point in worrying about it, and if it is in my control then there is no point in worrying about it." Also the book *Don't Sweat the Small Stuff and It's All Small Stuff* by Richard Carlson was influential in helping me to overcome the worry habit. He wrote, "So many spend so much of their life energy 'sweating the small stuff', that they completely lose touch with the magic and beauty of life."

Sometimes you have to stop worrying, wondering and doubting. Have faith that things will work out, maybe not as you planned, but just how it's meant to be. And as you start to overcome the worry habit and stop sweating the small stuff, your ability to experience joy rises.

When you become present and leave worries aside, you will be surprised by all the beauty surrounding you. You will feel you are part of creation, and life will start to make sense. As you live free of worry, your ripple effect will change and alter not only your world, but the world around you.

# 31

## NO REGRETS

$\mathcal{B}$ronnie Ware is an Australian palliative care nurse who spent several years caring for patients in the last twelve weeks of their lives. She recorded their dying epiphanies in a blog called *Inspiration and Chai*, which gathered so much attention that she put her observations into a book called *The Top Five Regrets of the Dying*.

Ware writes of the phenomenal clarity of vision that people gain at the end of their lives, and how we might learn from their wisdom. "When questioned about any regrets they had or anything they would do differently," she says, "common themes surfaced again and again."

This book had such a massive impact on me at the time I read it that I would like to share the top five regrets of the dying, as witnessed by Bronnie Ware with you.

## 1. I wish I'd had the courage to live a life true to myself, not the life others expected of me.

"This was the most common regret of all. When people realise that their life is almost over and look back clearly on it, it is easy to see how many dreams have gone unfulfilled. Most people had not honoured even a half of their dreams and had to die knowing that it was due to choices they had made, or not made. From the moment that you lose your health, it is too late. Health brings a freedom very few realise, until they no longer have it."

## 2. I wish I hadn't worked so hard.

"This came from every male patient that I nursed. They missed their children's youth and their partner's companionship. Women also spoke of this regret, but as most were from an older generation, many of the female patients had not been breadwinners. All of the men I nursed deeply regretted spending so much of their lives on the treadmill of a work existence."

Earning a living is important, but not to the exclusion of other things. To fully participate in all aspects of life, such as spending time with loved ones and enjoying meaningful activities, we should leave work at work. When we reach the end of our lives, it is not our work that matters, but the people we loved.

### 3. I wish I'd had the courage to express my feelings.

"Many people suppressed their feelings in order to keep peace with others. As a result, they settled for a mediocre existence and never became who they were truly capable of becoming. Many developed illnesses relating to the bitterness and resentment they carried as a result. When you change the way you are by speaking honestly, it will raise your relationships to a whole new and healthier level."

### 4. I wish I had stayed in touch with my friends.

"Often they would not truly realise the full benefits of old friends until their dying weeks and it was not always possible to track them down. Many had become so caught up in their own lives that they had let golden friendships slip by over the years. There were many deep regrets about not giving friendships the time and effort that they deserved. Everyone misses their friends when they are dying."

### 5. I wish that I had let myself be happier.

"This is a surprisingly common one. Many did not realise until the end that happiness is a choice. They had stayed stuck in old patterns and habits. Fear of change had them pretending to others, and to their selves, that they were content, when deep within, they longed to laugh properly and have silliness in their life again. When you are on your deathbed, what others think of you is a long way from your mind."

Remember:

Life is too short to wake up in the morning with regrets. So love the people who treat you right, and forget about the ones who don't. I believe that everything happens for a reason... if you get a chance, take it... and if it changes your life, then let it.

*"A man is not old until his regrets take the place of his dreams."*

*Yiddish Proverb*

# 32

## FORGIVENESS

*"Anger and bitterness are an acid that does more harm to the body in which it is stored than to the person on whom it is poured."*

*Mark Twain (1835-1910)*
*American author and lecturer*

*A*t some point in life, we all have been hurt. How we deal with that hurt is up to us. Some people stay stuck in bitterness and anger their entire lives and never move beyond the pain. By choosing to forgive, we release ourselves from the grip of resentment, allowing us to move forward with our lives.

When someone has hurt us, consciously or unconsciously, one of the most difficult things we have to face in resolving the situation is the act of forgiveness. Sometimes it feels like it's easier not to forgive and that the answer is to simply cut the person in question out of our lives. In some cases, ending the relationship may be the right thing to do, but even in that case, we will only be free if we have truly forgiven. If we harbour bitterness in our hearts against anyone, we only hurt ourselves because we are the ones harbouring the bitterness. Choosing to forgive is choosing to alleviate ourselves of that burden, choosing to be free of the past, and choosing not to perceive ourselves as victims.

One of the reasons that forgiveness can be so challenging is that we feel we are condoning the actions of the person who caused our suffering, but this is a misunderstanding. Forgiveness is something we do for ourselves, and our forgiveness of others is an extension of our readiness to let go of our own pain. We can choose to forgive someone even without their apology. Getting to this point begins with fully accepting what has happened. Through this acceptance, we allow ourselves to feel and process our emotions.

Whenever we hold onto our bitterness and anger, it invariably turns something small into something big in our mind. We start to believe that being right is more important than our happiness. It isn't. If you desire more peace in your life, then you need to understand that being right is never more important than allowing yourself to be happy. The way to happiness is to come from love, let go, and reach out. Let others be right. This doesn't mean that you are wrong. You'll experience the peace of letting go, as well as the joy of letting others be right. You'll notice that as you reach out, others will become less defensive and possibly more loving towards you. But, if for some reason they don't, that's okay too. You'll have the inner satisfaction of knowing that you have done your part to create a more loving relationship, and you will still have your peace.

Forgiving allows us to let go and be free again in our mind and heart. An open heart is a heart that is full of love; love for the self and love for all of humanity.

# 33

## MONEY AND WEALTH

*We* live in a society where success is often measured by how much money we earn. I feel our culture values money way too highly.

*The Sunday Times Rich List* is published every year, sending out the message that having more money than the next person is something to aspire to. This has led to a mentality where once we have grabbed hold of whatever money we can, we hold onto it as tightly as possible. This same culture says that if you give it away, then you will end up poor. But the little-known secret of money it that the opposite is true: it is only when a person starts to give away what they have, that they begin to gain riches far beyond just coins. In my experience, accumulating and clinging tightly on to money will never make you happy.

Money is like a river; it needs to flow or it will die. When you dam up a stream, the water soon becomes stagnant. Likewise with money: stop moving it along or giving it away and helping others, and the money starts to go stagnant. It's not how much money you have that matters, it's what you do with it. That's how you become really rich.

If you take a moment to consider your own feelings regarding money and wealth, you may discover that you equate financial prosperity with happiness, power, security, independence, or pleasure – I know I did. Money itself, however, is none of these things. Money is neutral.

You can begin developing a healthier view of wealth by simply accepting that we all have the potential to create lives of beauty, substance and wisdom using the resources we have been given.

Many believe that happiness is achieved through material wealth. I've learned that, yes, wealth is a tool that gives you choices – but it can't compensate for a life not fully lived, and it certainly can't create a sense of peace within you. A rich person is not someone who has more, but someone who desires less. Happiness is the result of total appreciation of all that life gives you at every moment. I learned many great wealth principles from *Think and Grow Rich* by Napoleon Hill and *The Richest Man in Babylon* by George S. Clason.

I hope the way you spend your money is in line with the truth of who you are and what you care about. I hope that your money brings joy to you and your loved ones. And I hope you use it as a powerful force for good to fulfil your best intentions.

These days, everyone's telling you to invest your money because of rising inflation caused by the pandemic. But if you're new to the game, investing your hard-earned money is no easy choice. The truth is, there are very few investments with low risks and high returns.

But there is one way to invest your time, energy, and money that'll always be worth it: an investment in yourself. Invest in your mind by learning new skills. Invest in your health by taking more time to move your body and prepare nourishing meals. Invest in **yourself** by spending more time around people who make your heart dance. Invest in experiences you're genuinely excited about.

The greatest wealth is to appreciate what we have and what we are.

*"Some people are so poor, all they have is money."*

*Anonymous*

# 34

## THE GOLDEN BUDDHA WITHIN

*I*n Bangkok there is a golden statue of the Buddha that stands 9'8" tall, weighs 5.5 tons, and the gold in the statue is worth approximately £250 million.

The statue was thought to have been built in 1403 and was revered by Buddhists for many hundreds of years. In 1757 the Burmese Army was invading Thailand. Facing complete annihilation, the Buddhist monks at the monastery hastily began covering their Golden Buddha with plaster and clay, which was painted and inlaid with bits of coloured glass, to make it look of little or no value to the invading army. During the invasion all the Buddhist monks were tragically murdered, but the Golden Buddha was left undiscovered.

The statue then survived centuries of storms, changes of government and political turmoil. Although the statue wasn't particularly beautiful, it was deeply revered. In its presence, people felt a soothing sense of comfort, of familiarity.

In 1957, the time came for the Monastery to receive some renovations. In preparation, the monks were preparing to move the statue. It was dry season and the air was particularly hot and arid. As the process began, one monk noticed a large crack on the surface of the statue. Curious, he beamed a light inside. Upon peering in, he discovered a golden light emanating from the crack. Immediately, he shared his discovery with his fellow monks. Shortly after, a group of them gathered with hammers and chisels to chip away at the plaster and clay. Soon, the group's efforts revealed a great, great treasure: the largest golden statue of the Buddha known to exist today.

What I love about this story is that the statue was purposely covered over with plaster and clay so it could survive difficult times. Much in the same way, we cover our own innate well-being with defence strategies and coping mechanisms in order to survive our difficult times.

We are all like the golden Buddha. When we are born, we are pure, intuitive, and we shine with light. As we grow, we throw on layers of stories from other people's ideas and opinions; we buy into the belief that we are broken. We doubt our intuitive insights, and we start to cover up the golden light that is within us. We constantly buy products to make us feel better and worthier. We speak quietly and don't voice our opinions and beliefs so as not to disappoint those around us. We buy the clothes and cars we believe we should want, and we pursue the friendships we think we need to make us feel valid. We allow negative emotions like anger, resentment, doubt, and fear to hide our true nature, even from ourselves. We are so laden with clay we have forgotten our golden Buddha within.

What this story highlights for me is that the issue is not that we have the covering, but our relationship to it. Pain and suffering are natural and inevitable parts of being a living, breathing, feeling human being. In fact, the habit patterns we adopt are a mere reflection of our instinctive desire to survive in the best way we know. The issue arises when we get so identified with the covering, that we forget our own true self that is glimmering underneath.

In my experience, staying connected to the essence of who we are is the key to cultivating the patience, understanding and self-compassion necessary for turning our gaze inwards. As we do so, some of the habit patterns we learnt in the past, that are no longer useful in the present moment, start to drop away.

By peeling away this covering, we reveal that all the treasures we seek are not outside but are within ourselves. We already have everything we need.

Don't be afraid to be amazing!

# 35

## DO YOUR BEST

Your best is always good enough, because it comes from you, and you are always good enough. We often come into contact with the idea that our best isn't good enough, as if this were actually possible. If you examine this notion, you will begin to see that it doesn't make much sense. You may not be able to deliver someone else's idea of the best, but the good news is that's not your burden. You only need to fulfil your own potential, and as long as you remain true to that calling, and always do your best to fulfil your purpose, you don't need to expect anything more from yourself.

It's easy to get tangled up with the idea of trying to be the best – the best parent, the best employee, the best child, or best friend. If we try to be the best, we run the risk of short-circuiting our originality because we are striving to fit into someone else's vision of success. However, there is nothing wrong with wanting to improve, but examining where this feeling comes from is important because wanting to be better than others, is our ego coming into play.

When I am trying to be the best, by doing everything, by striving to beat others, I have noticed that I never feel enough. A good part of our motivation to do everything is that we feel we should be doing more. We should be doing better. We are missing out. We should be living life differently. And so we try to do more, do better, do it all. And that still leaves us feeling like we're not enough, because when we're motivated by that feeling; there can never be an end to it.

Every day, we either encourage or discourage ourselves when it comes to our work, our goals, our habits, our self-care and exercise. I have trained myself to encourage myself through my self-talk. Most people have been trained to be discouraging. "I can't do this, I'm not disciplined, I don't trust myself, I keep messing up, and it's too hard." It's like having a coach tell you you're rubbish and pointing out everything you've done wrong, over and over again. Encouragement is what we need. "I can do this, I just need to make a little progress, keep going, don't quit, love yourself, you are a good person, and you've got this."

What if we could just start to see ourselves as already enough? Love who we already are? Be in love with ourselves and life, just as we are, just as life is right now?

Letting go of the tendency to hold ourselves up to other people's standards, and letting go of the belief that we need to compete and win, doesn't mean we don't believe in doing the best we can. We always strive to do our best, because when we do we create a life free of regret, knowing we have performed to the best of our ability. This allows us to feel great personal satisfaction in all of our efforts, regardless of how others perceive the outcome.

When you do your best, you learn to accept yourself. But you have to be aware and learn from your mistakes. Learning from your mistakes means that you practice, look honestly at the results, and keep practicing. Everything you have ever learned, you learned through repetition. If you do your best always, over and over again, you will become a master of transformation.

You are the artist of your own life; don't give the paint brush to anyone else.

# 36

## ENOUGH

*I*f like me you watch TV and read books about business or sports, you often see the world framed as a place where everyone wants "more, more and more". The old car bumper sticker from the eighties sums it up: "Whoever dies with the most toys, wins." The potent but usually unstated message is that we are all trapped in a lifelong contest where people can never get enough money, prestige, victories, cool stuff, beauty, or sex – and that we do and should want more goodies than everyone else.

This attitude fuels a quest for constant improvement that does have an upside, leading to anything from more functional products, to better surgical procedures and medicines, to more effective organisations. Yet when taken too far, this blend of constant dissatisfaction and competitiveness can damage your mental health. It can lead you to treat those "below" you as inferior and people "above" you who have more possessions and status, as objects of your envy.

Certainly, some people need more than they currently have, as many people on earth still need a safe place to live, enough good food to eat and fresh water to drink. But too many of us are never satisfied and are constantly striving, even though we have all we need to live a good life.

In the not too distant past, I too was guilty of this until I read a lovely little story that the American writer Kurt Vonnegut published in *The New Yorker* called *Joe Heller*. It is about the author of the renowned World War II novel *Catch-22*, Joseph Heller.

> "Heller, an important and funny writer, now dead, and I were at a party given by a billionaire on Shelter Island. I said, "Joe, how does it make you feel to know that our host only yesterday may have made more money than your novel *Catch-22* earned in its entire history?"
>
> And Joe said, "I've got something he can never have."
>
> And I said, "What on earth could that be, Joe?"
>
> And Joe said, "The knowledge that I've got enough.""

What a great story! As I reflected on the underused word "Enough", I had a life-changing insight. For me, the message in Joe's story is that I am trapped in a lifelong infinite contest where I can never get enough money, things, properties, attention, appreciation, blessings, awards, recognition, and toys. I will just not be satisfied. For, I do not understand the word – Enough.

Adverts and social media used to make me believe I hadn't arrived in life if I haven't got the latest gadget or the newest car. Joe's story made me recognise that I have been given so much in my own life. There are so many areas in my life where I should heed his message. Here is a small list that I made.

- Family – Enough
- Good friends – Enough
- Love – Enough
- Home – Enough
- Business – Enough
- Memories – Enough
- Inspiration – Enough
- Recognition – Enough
- Opportunities – Enough
- Mentors – Enough
- Time – Enough
- Money – Enough

In the making of my list I also realised, **I am Enough**.

What are your thoughts on 'enough'?

*"Gratitude turns whatever we have into enough"*
*Buddha (c 563 BCE – c 483 BCE)*
*Founder of Buddhism*

# 37

## LIVING FROM THE INSIDE OUT

*"A man will be imprisoned in a room with a door
that's unlocked and opens inwards
as long as it does not occur to him to pull rather than push."*

*Ludwig Wittgenstein (1889-1951)
Austrian-British philosopher*

*L*iving from the inside out isn't just a revolutionary concept – it's a truth about the way life works. In a nutshell, 100% of your experience of life is created from the inside out. We move through life feeling our thinking about the outside world. And it feels like real life.

When I say 100% of our experience, I mean everything; from our work satisfaction, to our relationships, to our views on failure and success. That old saying that money can't buy happiness? Well it's true! And neither can the perfect partner, a jackpot lottery win, or the gleaming red Ferrari. Because nothing from the outside world can give us happiness. But our thinking about those things can. Which is why that feeling of happiness can be so fleeting.

When you feel any feeling at all, no matter how much it seems to be caused by an external circumstance, it is always coming from you. Actually, it's coming from your thoughts about the circumstance. The mind only works in one direction, from the inside out.

This is the opposite of everything we have ever been taught. The majority of us have been taught about an outside in model. That our outside world creates how we feel inside. What makes it even more confusing is that it really looks to us like our feelings are caused by circumstances. We may feel hurt when someone says something mean to us. We may feel sad when we experience a loss of something or someone. We may feel excited when we receive a compliment from a friend or stranger.

You may think there are lots of times when your circumstances changed and the way you felt changed at the same time. You may say, for example, "I used to always be worried about money. Then I inherited some money, and now I'm not worried about it." That may be true, but when you look closer, you see that it wasn't the money that gave you more contentment. It was the fact you were no longer thinking worried thoughts about money. So you had been living with the feeling of concern about money through your concerned thoughts. Then, circumstances changed and you were no longer thinking those concerned thoughts, and the feeling of concern disappeared.

I know this is true as I personally know several wealthy people who are still thinking worried thoughts about money. This also explains why there are so many depressed and unhappy millionaires in the world. And why there may be just as many joyful people living below the poverty line.

Most people think that experience is coming at them from the outside in, but it's actually coming through them from the inside out. Outside circumstances are actually neutral. What we think about a given circumstance determines what we feel, and this looks like reality to us. We're living in the feeling of our thinking, not the feeling of our world. Thought is the invisible middleman between circumstance and experience that shapes the perception of our life. The more we understand where our experience is coming from, the less frightened we'll be of that experience.

> *"If the only thing that people learned*
> *was not to be afraid of their experience,*
> *that alone would change the world."*
>
> *Sydney Banks (1931-2009)*
> *Philosopher and lecturer*

# 38

## THE SECRET OF THOUGHT

*R*ecently, I came across a letter from a wonderful teacher and mentor of mine called Mavis Karn. She became well-known for a letter she wrote back in 1998, entitled *The Secret*, which was a gift she gave to a group of young incarcerated boys she had worked with for over two years. When the prison project was coming to an end, Mavis wanted to provide the boys with something to remind them of what they had learned during their time together.

Amongst the many things Mavis shared with them, was how their experience of life was created via their thinking in the moment. She taught them that they weren't their mistakes, their past, or their diagnosis. Mavis explained to them that they were designed perfectly, with everything they needed inside of them. She pointed them back home to who they were at their essence, which is pure love and pure potential.

The letter was such a hit amongst the young boys that they made a poster out of it. Before long, it made its way into the adult prison. The message of hope and possibility was precisely what the rest of the prison population needed to hear. In typical Mavis fashion, she doesn't take credit for the contents of the letter. She said the letter wrote itself. She doesn't lay claim to it and is happy to share with whoever may benefit from it.

She expresses what she calls "the secret of thought" so beautifully I wanted to share it with everyone.

Here is how to read this letter.

1. Read it without trying to 'get it'. Let whatever thoughts and feelings come to you while reading this letter come to you with no filter or judgement.

2. Allow the feeling of the words to soak into you, like taking a relaxing bath at the end of a long, busy day.

3. Read it with a quiet mind.

## The Secret

Dear Kids (and former kids),

I have a secret to tell you. Nobody meant to keep it from you... It's just that it's been one of those things that's so obvious that people couldn't see it... like looking all over for the key that you have in your hand.

The secret is that you are already a completely whole, perfect person. You are not damaged goods, you are not incomplete, you are not flawed, you are not unfinished, you do not need remodelling, fixing, polishing or major rehabilitation. You already have within you everything you need to live a wonderful life. You have common sense, wisdom, genius creativity, humour, self-esteem... you are pure potential... you are missing nothing.

The only thing that can keep you from enjoying all that you already are, is a thought. One thought, your thought. Not someone else's thought. Your thought... Whatever thought you are thinking at the moment that feels more important to think than feeling grateful, alive, content, joyful, optimistic, loving and at peace... that's the only thing that's between you and happiness.

And guess who's in charge of your thinking? Guess who gets to decide where your attention goes? Guess who gets to write, produce, direct and star in the moment you're in the middle of? You! Just you. Not your past (stored thought), not the future (did you ever notice that it never, ever shows up?), not your parents (they all think their own thoughts), or your friends (ditto), or school or television or situations or circumstances or anything else. Just you.

Thinking is an awesome capability. Like any capability, it can be used, whether as a tool or as a weapon against ourselves and others. And just like with any other tool, we can tell whether we're using it for or against ourselves by how it feels. When we think against ourselves or others, we get in trouble. When we don't, we usually stay out of trouble.

*Feelings exist to warn us away from using our thinking to create trouble in our lives, and to guide us back to our natural, healthy ability to live our lives to the fullest.*

So, please remember that your thoughts are not always telling you the truth. When we're in low moods, feeling down, our thoughts are not to be trusted... our IQ drops. When our thoughts pass and we lighten up, our thinking is once again creative, positive... our IQ goes up. The only way you can feel badly about yourself and your life is if you think badly about them... it's up to you, every single minute you're alive. It's always up to you!

This is the best, most liberating secret I ever learned, and I want you to know it too.

With love,

Mavis

# 39

## STUDY CHILDREN

*Y*oung children are filled with divine spiritual wisdom. I encourage you to spend as much quality time with these new arrivals as possible! Get down on the floor and be with them at their level, as I have done so often myself. Look them directly in the eye and listen to them not as an equal, but as a student inquiring of a spiritual master.

Throughout my life I have always opted for the company of children over small talk from adults. Playing with toddlers has always brought me so much joy. The great Russian novelist Fyodor Dostoevsky once said, "The soul is healed by being with children." I believe this is so because they are so new to the world and far less burdened with preconceived notions about the people, situations, and objects they encounter. They do not avoid people on the basis of appearance, nor do they regard shoes as having only one function. They can be fascinated for half an hour with a pot and a lid, and they think anything is possible. They live their lives fully immersed in the present moment. This enables them to inhabit a state of spontaneity, curiosity, and pure excitement about the world that we, as adults, have a hard time remembering. Yet almost every spiritual path calls us to rediscover this way of seeing. In this sense, children are truly our gurus. They live from their soul and, by doing so, remind us adults about who we truly are – that is, spiritual beings having a temporary human experience, rather than the reverse.

I was blessed recently to take my two beautiful granddaughters down to my local park for a couple of hours. I say blessed because firstly it was lovely to spend quality time with just them, and secondly because it gave me time to study a park full of young children. It reminded me that we were all children at one time. Here's what I observed.

Children naturally get along with one another. They may have occasional disputes and arguments, but they usually end up finding ways to have fun together. They don't dwell on mistakes, and yet they have a tremendous ability to learn from anything and anyone. They go with the flow of life and treat everyone equally; they don't care if you are black, white or disabled. They constantly see the beauty in life; nearly everything is a potential source of joy and laughter. Children don't base their happiness on the size of their bank accounts or the size of their parents' bank accounts. They are open to new ideas. When you tell a child that they can't do something, they just look for something else they can do. These are all the natural qualities that everyone brings to life. They are qualities that can be regained by simply seeing that the only obstacle to them is our own thinking.

Does this mean that children are always happy? Absolutely not! Children can have big tempers, they can be very selfish and they can sulk over almost anything. Children are not always happy because they are human beings. They, like everyone else, react to their own thinking. The difference between children and most adults is that when children get upset they simply get upset and then go on with their lives. They don't label themselves as depressed or angry people. Although their thinking made them upset to begin with, they don't compound the problem by using their thinking to hold their negative feelings in place. The details of the upset aren't important to a child. Whether it was an argument with a sibling or a parent, or something that they attempted to do that failed, isn't relevant to a child. What is important is that they don't hold onto the memory as if it were happening right now.

While none of us are always happy, we were born with a natural curiosity, a desire to grow and learn. We were born with an open and accepting attitude, and an innocent and healthy sense of humour. We were born seeing the beauty in our surroundings. If we remove our veil of negative thinking by recognising that thoughts are just thoughts, and by ignoring our negative thoughts, we will redevelop this childlike attitude, then we will feel good again.

I encourage you to study young children as they can be our greatest teachers.

# 40

## WHAT OTHER PEOPLE THINK OF ME IS NONE OF MY BUSINESS

*"What other people think of me is none of my business. One of the highest places you can get to is being independent of the good opinions of other people."*

Dr Wayne Dyer (1940-2015)
*American spiritual author and motivational teacher*

*I* used to worry a lot about what other people thought about me. I would get consumed by it and play lots of different variations out in my head, which could take up hours in my day. Eventually, I came to the realisations I share below. These are what made the change for me. They switched off that "Oh what are they thinking?" switch in my head.

But let's start at the beginning. It all started at school, as I'm sure it does for most of us. School is a period in your life where you are almost solely preoccupied with what other people think about you. "What's cool?", "What do they think about my hair?", "What do they think about my clothes, or my trainers?", "Oh, I hope they like me."

This continues even after school. In college or university, you want to be invited to all the parties; you are wondering what that cute girl at the other end of the room thinks about you... "Does she like me? Does she think I'm cute? Should I go over there and talk to her?" Later on, you worry about what your boss thinks, what your kids think, what the random stranger across from you on the train thinks about you...

I'm here to tell you a little secret.

What they think about you really does not matter. The only thing that matters is what you think about yourself.

We cannot read people's minds. So why do we all act like we can? We assume we know what people are saying... "Oh they all hate my dress!"... or that you know they are thinking... "Oh they all think I'm fat!" I'm sorry to break the news to you but that is just you deciding for them what they are thinking or saying. So the first lesson I learned was that I was probably making the wrong assumptions.

Our own thoughts are the only thing that matter. When we are preoccupied with what other people think, we are not aware of our own thoughts. We are trying to achieve what we think other people think we should achieve. We can't control what they are thinking or why they are thinking it. Everyone has their own lives and own reasons for reacting the way they do. The only person you really know and whose opinion really matters is yourself.

We are often living either in the future, in the past or trying to live in someone else's mind. When we worry about what other people think, we will never really focus on what we want in life. Happiness isn't achieving someone else's ideals, but achieving what is important to us. Start focusing on what you enjoy in life.

Do you know what happens when you decide to stop worrying about what other people might think of you?

You get to dance.

You get to sing.

You get to laugh loudly, paint, write, and create.

You get to be yourself.

And you know what? Some people won't like you. Some will laugh or mock or point out flaws…but it just won't bother you all that much.

# 41

## JUDGE LESS, ACCEPT MORE

*R*ecently I was at a retreat with twenty other people, seventeen of whom I had never previously met. Within ten minutes of sitting waiting for the event to start, I realised I had made judgements on more than half the group. This was before anyone had even spoken! It made me realise just how much I judge people in everyday life. During the course of the weekend I became aware that every one of my prior judgements was completely wrong! I was immensely grateful for this insight as now I am aware of it, I feel that I judge less and accept more.

Though it is human to evaluate people we encounter based on first impressions, the conclusions we come to are influenced by our own preconceptions, and our judgements are frequently incorrect. At the heart of the tendency to categorise and criticise, we often find our own insecurity.

When we catch ourselves thinking or behaving judgementally, we should ask ourselves where these judgements come from. Traits we hope we do not possess can instigate our criticism when we see them in others because passing judgement distances us from those traits. To acknowledge to ourselves that we have judged is the first step on the path of compassion. Recognising that we limit our awareness by assessing others critically, can make moving past our initial impressions much easier. Judgements never leave room for alternate possibilities.

If we are quick to pass judgement on others, we forget that they, like us, are human beings. As we seldom know what roads people have travelled before a shared encounter or why they have come into our lives, we should always give those we meet the gift of an open heart. Doing so allows us to replace fear-based criticism with acceptance and compassion, because we can then focus wholeheartedly on the spark of good that burns in all human souls.

We all find occasion to judge, to reject and resist other people. We all like to put up a fight against anything we dislike on the evening news as we watch the world. But we forget that when we decide we will resist something or somebody, either mentally or physically, we only empower the object of our resistance, either in reality or in our own minds.

I recently realised that this all also applies to me. I am always quick to pass judgement on myself; in fact, at times I judge myself, my thoughts and actions, more than I do anyone else. Why don't we all practice unconditionally accepting ourselves for the amazing human beings that we all are?!

# 42

## SEPARATE REALITIES

$\mathcal{I}$t's only recently, with the benefit of understanding how the mind works, that I now truly understand that we all live in separate realities. Essentially, this means that because we all think uniquely, we each live in a separate psychological reality.

As we grow up we learn to take everything personally. We think we are responsible for everything. Nothing other people do is because of you. It is because of them. All people live in their own reality, in their own mind; they are in a completely different world from the one you live in. When you take things personally, you feel offended, and your reaction is to defend your beliefs which can create conflict. You make something big out of something small, because you have the need to be right and make everybody else wrong.

You try hard to be right by giving them your own opinions. But what you say and do, and the opinions you have, are according to your beliefs, and these opinions are just your point of view, something personal to you. It's no one's truth but yours. In the same way, others are going to have their own opinions according to their beliefs. Nothing they think about me is really about me; it is about them. The understanding of this principle literally changed my life; I used to think that most people thought the same way as I did, and if they didn't then they should, or they were in some way wrong. But once I understood the principle that it is about them, I started to notice my habit of taking things personally starting to drop away.

When we expect to see things differently, when we accept that others will do things differently and react differently to the same things, the compassion we have for ourselves and for others rises dramatically. The moment we expect otherwise, the potential for conflict exists. We are only ever experiencing life through our thinking; no two people are ever going to have the same experience. Going on a long walk in any weather for me is a wonderful experience; for some of my friends, it would be a nightmarish experience, especially if it were to rain. Same event, two very different experiences.

Our experiences of each other changes once we see that we're all living in separate realities. Just notice in your day-to-day life how people react so differently to events happening all around us. What is the truth? What's real? When we can see that the events themselves, whether that's a conversation, a text message, a meal out, a colleague's behaviour, are neutral until we give them meaning, then we can step back and not get so anxious and caught up. Our thinking alone and our consciousness which brings it all to life, is the only thing causing us to feel either delight or anger, or any other emotion.

This one is easy to apply. All you have to do is expect, rather than be surprised or disappointed, when someone disagrees with you or can't see things your way. Of course they can't! Remember, we all live in separate realities. Make it a habit not to take anything personally, then you won't need to place your trust in what others do or say.

I encourage you to consider deeply and respect the fact that we are all very different. When you do, the love you feel for others as well as the appreciation you have for your own uniqueness will grow.

There are 7.6 billion people on this planet all experiencing life in a different way. That's both mind-blowing and humbling.

# 43

## THE ENERGY OF LOVE

*I* recently attended a retreat up in the Lake District titled "For the Love of Life". That weekend, something shifted in me that allowed me to understand the energy of love.

I have never wanted to talk about this energy of love. It seemed silly to my ego. I had started to get fed up with the clichés surrounding it: "Love is all you need... Love conquers all... Love will set you free." Yet after my retreat experience, I now know the truth of this energy. All I want to do is experience more of this and point others towards it.

This energy of love is a positive feeling that comes in many disguises. It may be the feeling of seeing a baby smile or a child playing with her new puppy, it may be a doctor caring for his patient, a father playing football with his children, it may be caring for and helping a neighbour, or it may be bringing a little joy to others who are less fortunate. We can experience it in so many ways. When watching a beautiful sunset or sunrise. Tasting a delicious meal cooked by someone who made it with care and the freshest ingredients. Feeling the warm smile of a stranger passing you on the riverbank. Or it may be laughing so hard with a friend that your stomach hurts.

I realised that what I have always wanted to do is rediscover this universal love. I believe it is what we all long for, why we do everything we do. We all want to experience this feeling of love.

I am learning that when people bring this energy to what they do, magic happens. Conflicts resolve, creation happens and life becomes easy, rich and beautiful. I have come to understand that when we stop thinking, we return to our true nature. Our true nature is part of this universal intelligence that creates all of life. Returning to our true nature is so magnificent. I really can't even begin to describe it. The feeling is so wonderful. It leaves me speechless and filled with a deep joy. When we are connected to our true nature, we will know what to do, when to do it, what to say, and how to say it.

The experience of love is one of the best things in life. When you love someone, let both your words and deeds be love. No one is promised tomorrow, so tell your loved ones each day how much they mean to you. Not only will your relationships grow, you will as well.

Love is not just an idea; love is a living, breathing essence.

Love makes the impossible possible.

# 44

## THE WISDOM WITHIN FEAR

*A*nything worth doing will always have some fear attached to it; it will invariably involve change, sometimes major change. I have constantly resisted change in my lifetime only to recently realise that the only thing we can guarantee in our lives **is** change.

For example, having a baby, getting married, changing careers, starting your own business – all of these life changes can bring up deep fears. It helps to remember that this type of fear is good. It is our way of questioning whether we really want the new life these changes will bring. It is also a potent reminder that releasing and grieving the past is a necessary part of moving into the new.

Fear has a way of throwing us off balance, making us feel uncertain and insecure, but it is not meant to discourage us. Its purpose is to notify us that we are at the edge of our comfort zone, poised in between the old life and a new one. Whenever we face our fear, we overcome an inner obstacle and move into new and life-enhancing territory, both inside and out. The more we learn to respect and even welcome fear, the more we will be able to hear its wisdom, wisdom that will let us know that the time has come to move forward, or not. While comfort with fear is a contradiction in terms, we can learn to honour our fear, recognising its arrival, listening to its intelligence, and respecting it as a signal of transformation. Indeed, it informs us that the change we are contemplating is significant, enabling us to approach it with the proper respect.

Fear of the future used to paralyse me, preventing me from living in the moment and from working toward my purpose. For me, awareness was the key to start conquering my fears. I started with the awareness that the universe would not present me with any circumstances that I am not capable of handling. And then I realised that when I am present I have no future thoughts. Fear of the future can paralyse us, but we can allow it to unfold easily when we keep to the present moment. When you can identify the irrational thoughts that frighten you, you can replace them with logical, self-affirming ideas.

Should fear of the future strike you as you strive to create, to excel, to grow, and to evolve, assert your courage. Assume that your fear is based on a false assumption and return to the present moment. Try to disregard past patterns and focus on the present by stilling the inner voice that comments critically on all you do. Tell yourself that the inevitability of your success is based not on luck or a universal mistake but on your already established talents, drive, imagination, and inner strength. Each time you overcome your fear of the future, you chip away at its very foundations. Remember that fear almost always comes alongside anything worth doing in your life.

*"When we are no longer able to change a situation,*
*we are challenged to change ourselves."*

*Viktor Frankl (1905-1997)*
*Austrian philosopher, author*
*and Holocaust survivor*

# 45

## WHAT MATTERS MOST

$\mathcal{O}$ne of the most significant lessons I learned in life is valuing what really matters most. I used to think that money, status, and wealth mattered most in life, but my reality is now very different.

Nothing will ever be more important than the people you love and the experiences you'll have in your life. While money and wealth may be significant, love and time are even more important in life. Family, friends, relationships, time, memories, and experiences are what truly matter to me, along with my purpose which gives me direction, and my continued good health.

It's easy to get lost and overwhelmed in the chaos, responsibilities, and goals of life. And once we are overwhelmed, we tend to forget about or postpone the things that are really important to us. Every day there will be lots of things that say, "I am important, you need to worry about me." Your job is to look away from these things and look towards your heart to see what is important to you. I've found it really helpful to constantly keep asking myself, "What really matters?" I feel we all need reminders to do what matters most to us and to let go of what doesn't matter.

As part of my early morning routine, I take some time to ask myself this question. When I remind myself of what's really important, it helps me to stay focused on my priorities. It reminds me that, despite all my responsibilities, I have a choice where I put my greatest amount of energy – being available for my loved ones, writing, my inner work, my health and mental well-being.

Despite the fact that this all seems very simple, I have found this one question to be immensely helpful in keeping me on the right track. When I do take time to remind myself of what really matters, I find that I am more present and living in the now, in less of a rush, and more accepting of everything and everyone around me. The opposite of this is also true, when I forget to remind myself what really matters. I find that I lose my accepting feelings, get lost being busy, rush everywhere, start future thinking, and do other things that are in conflict with my priorities.

Imagine a life where all your time is spent on the things you want to do. If you regularly take time to check in with yourselves, to ask "What matters most?", you may find that some of the choices you are making are in conflict with your own priorities. This one question can help you arrange your actions with your priorities and support you to make more conscious, loving decisions.

*"What matters most is to focus on what matters most."*

*Roy T. Bennett (1957- )*
*American author and thought leader*

# 46

## 80/20 YOUR LIFE

*W*hat if you focused your life only on the activities, purchases, decisions, and behaviours that brought you the most happiness and satisfaction?

If you poured all of your actions and behaviours into a sieve and allowed the least vital stuff to fall through the holes, you'd have about 20% remaining. This is a real observable phenomenon known as Pareto's Law, or the 80/20 Rule. This rule suggests that 20% of anything is always responsible for 80% of the results. You can apply the 80/20 Rule to almost anything, from the science of management to the physical world. If you apply this principle to every aspect of your own life and focus with intensity on that 20%, you will find a better way to live.

Is that possible? One hundred percent! However, you have to plan for it and arrange your life to support it.

Think about these questions:

- How much space in your home do you really use?
- How many of your material possessions do you rarely or never use or notice?
- How much of your wardrobe do you never wear?
- How much of your time do you spend taking care of things you don't really enjoy?
- How much money do you spend on things that you could do without?
- How much of your effort in your job or business is really productive?
- How much of your "free" time is spent doing things you enjoy or that are uplifting?
- How much time do you spend on trivial tasks, errands, and driving?

This exercise forced me to embrace two facts:

1. I acknowledge that I can't have, be, or do everything in life, and I no longer want to attempt that. It's a waste of my time.

2. Since the start of the global pandemic in 2019, I've become more aware of what's most important to me, and so I decided to spend my time and energy on those things.

If this intrigues you, the place to start is with that ideal 20% in all areas of your life. Some of your existing top 20% might or might not be part of your ideal. The goal is to define the ideal and then shift out of most of the 80% of trivial pursuits and create the 20% to match your ideal.

Start by defining the kind of lifestyle you want. You'll need to figure out how to pay for this lifestyle, so you must first define it. You may discover that by paring it down to the most essential 20%, you will have more time and money to work with.

Take a good look at the home you are in. If it's possible that your home is causing you more stress, expense, and energy than it is giving you pleasure, then perhaps it's time to make a change. Look around you at your stuff. There are so many things in your home that you don't use or need; they seemed imperative at the time of purchase, but now they are just taking up space. It is hard to have unfettered happiness when you are surrounded by useless objects. They suck energy from you, consuming your attention and causing indecision and distraction. There are probably people all around you who would love your stuff. Let them have it!

You might be surprised when you design your life around your top 20% of activities and possessions; you may not need as much money as you do now. We fritter away money on useless purchases and activities all the time. Once you've set aside a budget for the most essential expenses (food, shelter, utilities, fuel, an emergency fund, and maybe a few others), create a lifestyle savings account to fund your top 20%.

Much of our unhappiness in life stems from feeling out of control. When we feel trapped by our circumstances, our stuff, or our work, we lose our ability to thrive. Set yourself free from the trivial in your life, and focus on the most productive, positive, and energising 20%. This can be a major component of a happy and flourishing life.

Pareto's rule of 80/20 tells us that 20% of our efforts give us 80% of our desired results. Figure out where the 20% is. Fast.

# 47

## KINDNESS

*I*ntentional kindness is life-giving. It works wonders in putting people at ease and improving relationships. A smile or a kind gesture can make someone's day brighter. Being kind is an easy practice that enhances our own lives and the lives of others, whether we know them or not.

Kindness is an ideal that is easily accessible to all of us. We all know that a small kindness can make our journeys lighter and more enjoyable. Even bringing an instance of kindness to mind can put a smile on your face days or weeks later, or perhaps even inspire you to share kindness with another.

For example, I was walking through the Winter Gardens in Bournemouth around midday on New Year's Eve; it was very busy with lots going on. As I walked through a maze of people, I noticed a young dishevelled girl sat on the ground with blankets around her. As I passed her, I couldn't help but make eye contact and as I did, she gave me this beautiful smile. I continued on down to the seafront where I walked for a couple of hours. On returning back through the gardens, I saw her again and although she did not appear to be begging I felt compelled to reach out to her with a gift of money. On receiving it, she totally lit up with a genuine heartfelt gratitude that I could actually feel. As I walked back to my car I wondered, who had made whose day? As I sit here a month later, I can still feel the gratitude and it brings a smile to my face.

Choose being kind over being right.

Choosing to be kind over being right has had a massive impact on my life whenever I remember it and act on it. The next time you have the chance to be right, to correct someone, even if their facts are a little off, resist the temptation. Instead, ask yourself, "What do I really want from this interaction?" Chances are what you really want is a peaceful interaction where you both end up feeling good. Each time you resist "being right" and instead choose kindness, you'll experience a peaceful feeling within.

In a way, kindness acts as the oil that makes the engine of our world move more smoothly and with less friction. We can still get where we are going but the ride is more pleasant, and those around us can share in the ideal world that we help to create. We are all fortunate that kindness is limitless in its supply and available to everyone.

Whether giving way to someone in traffic or letting someone go ahead of us in the queue, donating money or sharing our resources in a crisis, we actively create a universe of kindness and giving with every choice we make. The smallest gesture can bring a smile to light the shadow of an unpleasant situation or remove tension from a difficult task, but its effects can ripple out and extend far beyond the moment.

The thing about kindness is that it costs the giver very little but can mean the world to the receiver. We don't always see the results of what we do, but never underestimate the impact even just a small act of kindness has on the world.

Kindness in words creates confidence.

Kindness in giving creates love.

*"Apologising doesn't always mean that you're wrong and the other person is right. It just means that you value your relationship more than your ego."*

*Anonymous*

# 48

## CHOOSING NOT TO LOOK AWAY

$\mathcal{M}$ost of us know in our hearts that the homeless and the poor are not so very different from us.

Homeless people in our communities are a fact of life; there was a time when it was just in big cities, now it seems more widespread. My hometown of Wallingford – population around 12,000 – regularly has visible homeless people. Many of us don't know how to interpret this situation or what we can do to help. We may swing between feeling guilty, as if we are personally responsible, and feeling angry, as if it is entirely on their own shoulders. The situation is, of course, far more complex than either scenario. Still, not knowing how to respond, we may fall into the habit of not responding at all. We may look over their heads, not making eye contact, or look down at the ground as we pass, falling into a habit of judging and ignoring them. Each time we do this, we disconnect ourselves from a large portion of the human family, and it doesn't feel right.

They may be the victims of poor planning or an unavoidable crisis. Some of them are mentally ill, some are addicted to drugs or alcohol, and some are choosing to be homeless for reasons we may never understand. If we had their life experience, we could possibly have ended up in the same place. This does not mean that we are meant to rescue them, as they are on their own learning path, but it does remind us that we can treat them as equals, because that is what they are. Even if we aren't able to offer food, shelter, or money, we can offer a blessing as we pass. I sometimes give the gift of time, spending time just listening to them. We can look them in the eye and acknowledge our shared humanness, even if we don't know just how to help them. This simple act of kindness and silent or spoken blessings can be so helpful to those living in poverty on the street.

I used to be one of those people that would look away whenever possible. I'd be judging them in my head, thinking that if I did give them money they would only waste it on drink and/or drugs. I was coming from separation, thinking that we're not the same so why should I help? I had forgotten that we are all one, I had forgotten how when we help a fellow human feel better, we feel better.

Whatever you decide to do, you will feel much better when you make a conscious choice not to simply look away.

# 49

## IMPERFECTION

$\mathcal{I}$n our culture, we move relentlessly toward greater emphasis on achievement and goal orientation. When we do so, we seem to lose the capacity for wonder and awe. Could you imagine looking at a magnificent rainbow and complaining that one of the colours wasn't perfect? Not only would that be ridiculous, but we'd also be ruining the splendour of the moment. And yet that is exactly what we do when we judge ourselves for our imperfections. We forget that as humans, we're part of nature as well. As such, we would benefit if we came into acceptance of the natural state of life, which by the way happens to be imperfect.

Life becomes much more interesting once we let go of our quest for perfection and aspire for imperfection instead. For a major part of my life I have strived for perfection in all areas of my life. I now recognise that whenever I am attached to having something a certain way, better than it already is, I am fighting a losing battle. Rather than being content and grateful for what I have, I tend to focus on what's wrong with something and try and fix it.

Whether it's related to ourselves – a disorganised wardrobe, a dirty car, a missed opportunity at work, a few pounds we would like to lose – or someone else's imperfections – the way someone looks, behaves, or lives their life – the act of focusing on imperfection pulls us away from our goal of inner peace. When we make mistakes, we think that we are failing or not measuring up. But if life is about experimenting, experiencing, and learning, then to be imperfect is a must.

This doesn't mean that we don't strive to be our best. It's about realising that while there's always a better way to do something, this doesn't mean we can't appreciate and enjoy the way things already are.

All living things are in a ceaseless state of movement. Even as you read this, your hair is growing, your cells are dying and being reborn, and your blood is moving through your veins. Your life changes more than it stays the same; in fact, the only constant in life is change. Perfection may happen in a moment, but it will not last because it is an impermanent state. Trying to hold on to perfection or forcing it to happen causes frustration and unhappiness.

When I notice myself slipping back into the habit of trying to be perfect, I gently remind myself that life is okay the way it is, and so am I. I am exactly who I need to be.

The other thing that helps me is to look at my life and notice that no one is judging me to see whether or not I am perfect. Sometimes, perfectionism is a holdover from our childhood – an ideal we inherited from a demanding parent or parents. We are adults now, and we can choose to let go of the need to perform for someone else's approval. Similarly, we can choose to experience the universe as a loving place where we are free to be imperfect. Once we realise this, we can begin to take ourselves less seriously and have more fun.

As I started to let go of perfection, I also gave myself permission to take life less seriously. Life is far too short to be spent worrying about things that are beyond our control. Allow joy and fun to be part of your life each day. Being mindful and open to the good that is present in all situations can help us not to take life so seriously, and is a key ingredient to having a more enjoyable life.

Imperfection is inherent to being human, and as we begin to let go of our need for perfection in all areas of our lives, we will begin to discover the perfection in life itself.

# 50

## WELCOME FAILURE

*"If you really want to achieve your dreams - I mean really achieve them, not just daydream or talk about them - you've got to get out there and fail. Fail early, fail often, but always fail forward. Turn your mistakes into stepping-stones for success."*

*John C Maxwell (1947- )*
*American author, specialising in leadership*

The essence of man is imperfection. Know that you're going to make mistakes. The fellow who never makes a mistake takes his orders from one who does. Wake up and realise this: failure is simply a price we pay on our journey. I personally feel that welcoming failure should be taught in our schools.

Failure teaches us so much about ourselves, and about life, that we should welcome it. Nothing worthwhile is ever easy. Sometimes when you try to do something new, or something difficult, or unusual, you may meet resistance, rejection or disappointment.

All we need to do is to find a way to cope with failure. I do it now by seeing failure as a stepping stone on the path to where I want to go. Every time I fail, I know I am one step closer to my destination.

The last time you failed, did you stop trying because you failed, or did you fail because you stopped trying? I have to admit that I have failed in the past because I just stopped trying.

In life, the question is not if you will have problems, but how you are going to **deal** with your problems. All great adventures have risk and a chance of failure. That's the whole point – otherwise it isn't an adventure.

If the possibility of failure were erased, what would you attempt to achieve?

# 51

## MOODS

*O*ur moods can be extremely deceptive. When we're in a "good" mood, life generally looks pretty good. We have perspective and common sense. In good moods, most things seem positive and it all seems to flow. However, when we're in a "bad" mood, the exact same life looks drastically different. We have very little perspective; we take things personally, and often misinterpret those around us. All of a sudden, the partner we were so in love with is problematic, the car we drive doesn't look so good and our future looks less than promising.

But how can this be? While in a good mood, we're totally in love, the car we drive is absolutely perfect and our future looks great. I could give a hundred other examples, but I'm sure you get the point. Our life doesn't change – only our mood does. Knowing this changes everything. When we're down, we feel it and we make allowances for it. We don't take our own thinking very seriously at all. A low mood is just an unavoidable human condition that will pass with time if we leave it alone.

Acknowledge it's a waiting game. We wait until our mood returns to a better state before making important decisions. It's the same with other people. You begin to recognise when someone is in a low mood and when they are, you don't take what they say and do very seriously. It's really that simple. Everyone is subject to moods and when any of us are in a low mood, we will say and do things we wouldn't even consider while in a better frame of mind. Knowing this is a huge advantage. We learn to make allowances for others and their mood, and we get to practice empathy and compassion.

Get comfortable recognising when you feel in a low mood and be prepared to let those around you know as well. This may feel like a weakness but in truth it's strength. When do you suppose most people discuss their problems? While in a low mood of course, because that's when life has a sense of urgency. But ironically, we can't solve a problem when we're low because we have lost our wisdom, common sense and happiness. Remember, never make a big decision while in a low mood. But when our mood rises, we will have our wisdom back and life looks good again!

It is perfectly normal for all human beings to go up and down, to have both good days and bad days; hard days can sometimes be a great teacher when we stop for reflection.

The trick is to be grateful for our good moods and graceful in our low moods, not taking them too seriously. The next time you feel low, remind yourself, "This too shall pass," and it will.

# 52

## CONNECTING WITH NATURE

*"In every walk in nature,
one receives far more than he seeks."*

*John Muir (1838-1914)
Scottish-American naturalist
and environmental philosopher*

*B*eing in nature is one of the most effective and simple ways to enhance our own energy. Nature is the pure expression and manifestation of the life force energy. We can learn much wisdom from nature. We can connect with it any time we want to. Not only does nature ground us, which means feeling connected to the earth, but it also enhances our connection to our soul and intuition, so we feel in balance. Being at one with nature makes me realise I am made of the same energy as nature. We need to be grateful and respect and honour our connection.

It depends on where you live as to what kind of landscapes and nature you can experience. Wherever it is, it's good for you, it nourishes your soul. I am fortunate to live in Wallingford in Oxfordshire near the River Thames and most mornings I take full advantage of this by walking beside the river for at least an hour. I normally do this first thing as it's a lovely way to start my day; it helps to ground me as I connect with nature. Sometimes I get extra lucky; in this last month I have encountered a couple of green woodpeckers, a kingfisher, several herons, and a cormorant sitting atop a tall tree, wings fully open to dry himself, looking like a large black angel on top of a totem pole!

I also create an opportunity around once a month to walk alongside or actually on a beach [despite it being at least a three-hour round trip]. Whenever possible, I go barefoot to feel the sand and water on my feet. I love to breathe in the salty air as I listen to the magical sound of the ocean. On the beach, I regularly collect sea glass, shells and rocks that all seem to have a mystical energy about them. I now have sea glass, shells and rocks all around my house; they help to remind me of that seaside feeling.

Perhaps you live by a hillside or mountain where you can walk. When you do, stop to take time to sense your surroundings, and to experience the breathtaking views. Smell the fresh air and feel the earth or grass beneath your feet. Sit on the rocks and feel their energy in your hands and throughout your body. Connect with the trees around you and absorb their vibrations. Be aware how grounded and calm this can make you feel.

You may be lucky to live near a wood or even a forest that you can walk through. If so, try leaning against an old tree and feel its vibration. You can sense and feel what its energy is like. I have noticed that it's impossible to walk in the woods and be in a low mood at the same time.

Maybe you live in a big city where there isn't very much nature. If you have a park nearby, just walking through the park and pausing to take it all in will certainly do you some good. You may not be able to lean on trees, but you can stand near one or by flowers to experience their energy and take note of how it makes you feel.

You can also experience the same things and feelings with the beauty of a garden. Hold your hand up to a flower and sense its energy. If you are not in a position to be outdoors, you can make your connection even being indoors. Having plants and flowers indoors adds positive energy and enhances the atmosphere. Also, if you can look out the window and see a tree, flowers, or animals, you can make a connection. As you connect, sense how much better you feel.

Spending time connecting with nature nourishes the soul, reminds you that you are never truly alone, and renews you by attuning you to the earth's natural rhythms. Taking a walk under the stars or feeling the wind on your face may be all it takes for you to reconnect with nature.

Remember, you are as much a part of nature as are the leaves on a tree or water bubbling in a brook.

I feel blessed that I understood at a very early age the importance of connecting with nature. It helps me to feel at one with the world.

"*I believe in God, only I spell it Nature.*"

*Frank Lloyd Wright (1867–1959)*
*American architect, designer, and writer*

# 53

## SURRENDER LEADS TO FREEDOM

*You are born – what effort have you made to be born?*
*You grow – what effort have you made to grow?*
*You breathe – what effort have you made to breathe?*
*Everything moves on its own, so why bother?*
*Let life flow on its own, then you will be in let go.*
*Don't struggle and don't try to move upstream,*
*don't even try to swim; just float with the current*
*and let the current lead you where it leads.*
*Be like a white cloud moving in the sky -*
*no goal, going nowhere, just floating.*
*This floating is the ultimate flowering...*

*Chuang Tzu (369 BCE-286 BCE)*
*influential Chinese philosopher and writer*

*S*everal years ago I was on a flight to India when I read the above quote by Chuang Tzu. Not only did it speak to me but intuitively I knew it to be truth. I was attending a yoga retreat in Rishikesh, located in the foothills of the Himalayas in Northern India, with nineteen other students from around Europe. At dinner on the first night, one of the leaders of the retreat asked if anyone had anything inspirational they would like to share to set the mood for our two weeks. I went first and shared this quote, and on finishing I looked up to find not a dry eye around our huge dinner table, me included. I hope it speaks to you too.

The flow of the universe moves through everything. It's in the rocks that form, get pounded into dust, and is blown away, the sprouting of a summer flower born from a seed planted in the spring, the growth cycle that every human being goes through, and the current that takes us down our life's paths. When we surrender, we move with the flow, rather than resisting it; we are riding on the universal current that allows us to flow with life.

Many people live their lives struggling against this current. They try to use force or resistance to will their lives into happening the way they think it should. Others move with this flow like a sailor using the wind, trusting that the universe is taking them exactly where they need to be at all times. This flow is accessible to everyone because it moves through and around us. We are always riding this flow. It's just a matter of whether we are willing to go with it or resist it. Tapping into the flow is often a matter of letting go of the notion that we need to be in control at all times. The flow is always taking you where you need to go.

One of my biggest ongoing lessons during the past few years and during the pandemic has been to learn to let go of the need to control and to accept that the only constant is change... I am learning that when I let go of even the tiniest desire to control even the smallest of things, then I start to feel free.

I remind myself to surrender to the reality that life is exactly as it should be in this moment. Surrender is a state of living in the flow, trusting what is, and being open to serendipity and surprises. When we allow everything to be exactly as it is right now in this moment... that's all there is to do. When we let go of having to be in control and manipulate everything, we see the perfection in what is already there.

If we don't interfere, our life will play out exactly as it should. It needs no help from us. Start to surrender and just watch in wonder and amazement as it all just happens. Life is simple. Everything happens for you, not to you. Everything happens at exactly the right moment, neither too soon nor too late. You don't have to like it... it's just easier if you do.

When we surrender, when we go with the flow of things, we find ourselves at peace and at one with the whole universe.

The most amazing thing to realise is that in spite of any conditions you find yourself in, you are always whole and complete. There is nothing you have to do to be that way... that's freedom.

# 54

## LIFE – OUR PERFECT TEACHER

*A*ll the situations in our lives, from the insignificant to the major, teach us exactly what we need to be learning at any given time.

Everyone has their share of life lessons. How well you learn from them is up to you. When you choose to see the world as a classroom, you understand that all experiences are here to teach you something about yourself. Sometimes the hardest experiences are often the ones that teach us the most. And that your life's journey is about becoming more of who you are.

Many of us long to find a spiritual teacher or guru. We may feel unsure of how to practice our spirituality without one, or we may long for someone who has attained a higher level of insight to lead the way for us. Some of us have been looking for years, sometimes travelling halfway around the world all to no avail, leaving us feeling frustrated and even lost. The good news is that the greatest teacher you could ever want is always with you – that is your life.

The people and situations we encounter every day have much to teach us when we are open to receiving their wisdom. Often, we don't recognise our teachers because they may not look or act like our idea of a guru, yet they may embody great wisdom. Everyone in your life has come to teach you something. I am currently working with a wonderful coach in an area of my life. She is eighty-two years old and recently shared with me how blessed she feels to still be coaching so many people as she learns something from every one of her clients.

Patience, compassion, perseverance, honesty, resilience, letting go – all these are covered in the classroom of the teacher that is our life.

For example, I used to get really frustrated with supermarket queues to the extent that I actually walked away, leaving my shopping behind once or twice, storming off and blaming the shop assistant for intentionally serving customers slowly. As I started to ask myself the question, "What is this trying to teach me?" I found myself feeling compassion for the shop assistants acknowledging that they were doing their best. It also teaches me that queuing is an excellent opportunity to break my habit of feeling impatient.

Take some time each day to consider what our lives are trying to teach us at this time. A difficult phase in your relationship with your child may be teaching you to let go. The homeless person you see every day may be showing you the boundaries of your compassion and generosity. A spate of lost items may be asking you to be more present to physical reality. A fall or an accident may be telling you to slow down.

Trust your intuition on the nature of the lesson at hand; work at your own pace. Our life has all the answers.

# 55

## TRUST YOUR INTUITION

The dictionary definition of intuition is "a thing that one knows or considers likely from instinctive feeling rather than conscious reasoning". Some refer to it as our "sixth sense", common sense or our gut instinct. I refer to it as our "inner voice or our inner wisdom". I have known of this inner voice since my childhood.

Everyone has intuition, we just need to recognise it. Our intuition is our best source of guidance. Whereas rational decisions come from our thinking mind, our gut is that "all-knowing" part of us that if paid close attention to and acted on, will never lead us astray. How often have you said to yourself, "I knew I should have done that?" How often do you intuitively know something but allow yourself to think yourself out of it?

Trusting your intuition may be awkward at first, particularly if you grew up around people who taught you to look to others for answers. We each have exclusive access to our inner wisdom. All we have to do is remember how to listen to it. Remember to be patient as you relearn how to hear, receive, and follow your own guidance. If you are unsure about whether following your inner wisdom will prove reliable, you may want to think of a time when you trusted your own knowing and everything worked out. Recall how the answers came to you, how they felt in your body as you considered them, and what happened when you acted upon this guidance. Now, recall a time when you didn't trust yourself and the results didn't work out as you had hoped. Trusting your own guidance can help you avoid going against what you instinctively know is right for you.

Within each of us, there are numerous voices that compete for our attention. It can be difficult to decide which one to listen to, particularly when their messages are all quite different, sometimes conflicting, and even seductive. One voice, however, is the speaker of truth. Among all your inner voices, your true inner voice is the one which encourages you, gives you hope, and pushes you to trust and believe in yourself. Conflict within oneself is often caused by duelling voices inside of each one of us. Some of our voices, such as the naysayer or saboteur, can speak so loudly that they can drown out the voice of truth. Listening to your true inner voice – often the voice of understanding, support, and self-assurance – can help lessen and even resolve internal conflict.

Trusting our intuition means listening to and trusting that quiet inner voice that knows what actions need to be taken, or changes need to be made in your life. You may hear many voices as you get quiet, but the one you should pay attention to is the one that speaks to you with love, understanding, and compassion. It will bolster your spirits and urge you to go after your dreams. And it will never cause confusion, remind you of past mistakes, or cause you to doubt yourself. When we overcome our fear that our intuition will give us incorrect answers, if we can learn to trust it, our life will become the magical adventure it was meant to be. Trusting our intuition is like removing the barriers to enjoyment; it unlocks the wisdom of the universe.

The more you listen to and believe in what your true inner voice is telling you about your value and your potential, the stronger that voice will become. And the more you disregard the negative voices, the quieter those voices will become. Saying no to the voices that are judgemental and make you feel ashamed will help you stop being critical of your failures and afraid of success. Pay attention only to the calm thoughts that begin to surface. If you find that unusual yet loving thoughts are appearing in your mind, take note and take action. If, for example, you get the urge to write or call someone you love, go ahead and do it. If your intuition says you need to slow down or take more time for yourself, make it happen.

Trust your intuition. You don't need to justify or explain your feelings to anyone, just trust your own inner guidance; it always knows best.

# 56

## BEING TRULY THANKFUL

*"If the only prayer you ever say in your entire life is 'Thank You,' it will be enough."*

Meister Eckhart (1260-1328)
German theologian and philosopher

*O*ur gratitude deepens when we begin to be thankful for being alive and living the life we are living.

Often when we practice being thankful, we go through the process of counting our blessings, acknowledging the wonderful people, things and places that make up our reality. While it is fine to be grateful for the good fortune we have accumulated, true thankfulness stems from a powerful comprehension of the gift of simply being alive, and when we feel it, we feel it regardless of our circumstances. In this deep state of gratitude, we recognise the purity of the experience of being, in and of itself, and our thankfulness is part and parcel of our awareness that we are one with this great mystery that is life.

It is difficult for most of us to access this level of consciousness as we are very caught up in the ups and downs of our individual experiences in the world. The thing to remember about the world, though, is that it ebbs and flows, expands and contracts, gives and takes, and is, by its very nature, somewhat unreliable. If we only feel gratitude when it serves our desires, this is not true thankfulness. No one is exempt from the twists and turns of fate, which may, at any time, take the possessions, situations, and people we love away from us. Ironically, it is sometimes this kind of loss that awakens us to a thankfulness that goes deeper than just being grateful when things go our way. Illness and near-miss accidents can also serve as wake-up calls to the deeper realisation that we are truly lucky to be alive.

We do not have to wait to be shaken to experience this state of being truly thankful for our lives. Tuning in to our breath and making an effort to be fully present for a set period of time each day can do wonders for our ability to connect with true gratitude. We can also awaken ourselves with the intention to be more aware of the unconditional generosity of the life force that flows through us, regardless of our circumstances.

I have noticed that as I make more effort to be thankful for everything, I become less judgemental. We can't be judgemental and thankful at the same time. Even when we feel as though things aren't going well in our life, when we are having experiences in life we don't want, if we can find it in us to be thankful for what we do have, that's enough to create a miracle. Gratitude can change things that look unchangeable. And suddenly we start to find life is working out after all.

Today, take time to appreciate the gift and miracle of life and all its wonders. Count your blessings and be truly thankful for what you have. Being truly thankful and coming from gratitude is another of those great universal laws that always make you feel better.

# 57

## GIVING AND RECEIVING

The most difficult time to be generous is when we ourselves are feeling poor. While some of us have experienced actually being in the red financially, there are those of us who would feel broke even if we had a million pounds in the bank. Either way, as the old adage goes, it is always in giving that we receive, meaning that when we are living in a state of lack, the very gesture we may least want to give, is the very act that could help us create the abundance that we seek. One way to practice generosity is to give energy where it is needed. Giving money to a cause or person in need is one way to give energy. Giving attention, love, or a smile to another person are other acts of giving that we can offer.

Sometimes when we practice generosity, we practice it conditionally. We might be expecting to "receive back" from the person to whom we gave. We might even become angry or resentful if that person doesn't reciprocate. However, trust in the natural flow of energy, and you will find yourself practicing generosity with no strings attached. This is the purest form of giving. Remember that what you send out will always come back to you. Selflessly help a friend in need without expecting them to return the same favour in the same way, and know that you too will receive that support from the universe when you need it. Besides, while giving conditionally creates stress (because we are waiting with an invisible balance sheet to be completed), giving unconditionally creates and generates abundance. We give freely because we trust that there is always an unlimited supply.

Giving and receiving are part of the same cycle, and we each give and receive in our own ways. But we can lose our balance when we try to be too controlling on either side of the cycle. On the receiving end, we may feel that we don't deserve the effort made if what we gave was easy for us to give. But perhaps there is a different lesson there for us. We may be receiving not only gratitude, but a chance to see the world through the eyes of another. We may be learning that just because we gave easily, it doesn't diminish its value. Or perhaps the universe is giving us an example to hold close to our hearts, to encourage us on some future day when our own generous act of giving is not met with a visible act of receiving.

When we can allow ourselves to receive as well as give, we do our part to keep the channels of abundance open for ourselves and others. We live in a world of abundance. It's all right to give to others and it's also all right to accept what we need with grace and gratitude. This can be a hard one for some of us to get our head around. There was a time in my earlier days that I found it hard to even receive a compliment!

Sometimes we may find ourselves struggling to respond to others' gifts in the same ways – like responding to an expensive present with something equally expensive, or feeling like we have to do a favour for someone who has done a favour for us. But when these are done out of a sense of obligation, the energy changes from something that shares, to something that drains. If this sounds familiar, we can decide next time to allow ourselves to receive with open arms, minds and hearts and simply say thank you.

Accepting a person's gift is a gift in itself. Sincere appreciation for their acknowledgement and their effort joins our energy with theirs in the cycle of giving and receiving, and nurtures all involved. The truth of the matter is that simply by giving, I will receive all that I need. Giving is receiving.

Make today a day of giving unconditionally: give a smile; give a word of appreciation; give a thought of good wishes; give a twenty-second hug.

# 58

## TWENTY-SECOND HUGS

*A* twenty-second hug creates an open-hearted exchange of energy between two beings in the most beautiful way.

Trust me and try this with someone you love. I remember how sceptical I was when a spiritual teacher shared the power of a twenty-second hug with me. Despite my initial discomfort, it was an amazing connective experience that I now love to share with my loved ones. I was reminded of the power of hugs during the global pandemic; the fact that we were not meant to hug highlighted just how much I missed that connection.

The need to touch and be touched is established early in our lives as we develop and grow in the embrace of our mother's womb. Once we are born, separated from that sanctuary of connectivity, we begin to crave the physical embrace of our parents. As we age, we become more independent. Yet during times of triumph or trouble and during those moments when we are in need of reassurance, we can't help but long for a hug.

Since a hug requires two active participants, each individual taking part in the embrace experiences the pleasure of being embraced and the joy that comes from hugging someone. As both individuals wrap their arms around one another, their energy blends together, and they experience a tangible feeling of togetherness that lingers long after physical contact has been broken. A heart hug is when you put your left arm over someone's shoulder and your right arm around their waist. As they do the same to you, your hearts become aligned with one another and loving, comforting energy flows between the two of you to flood your souls with feelings of love, caring, and compassion.

A hug is a pleasurable way to share your feelings with someone who is important to you. Depending on your relationship with the other person and the kind of message you wish to send them, a hug can communicate love, friendship, romance, congratulations, support, greetings and any other sentiment you wish to convey. A hug communicates to others that you are there for them in a positive way. In an instant, a hug can re-establish a bond between long-lost friends and comfort those in pain. The next time you hug someone, focus all of your energy into the embrace. You will create a profound connection that infuses your feelings and sentiments into a single beautiful gesture.

# 59

## THE TRUE SEVEN WONDERS OF THE WORLD

*O*ver the years, stories have been some of my greatest teachers and I feel it's fitting to finish the book with one of my all-time favourites.

Junior high school students in Chicago were studying the Seven Wonders of the World. At the end of the lesson, the students were asked to list what they considered to be the Seven Wonders of the World. Though there was some disagreement, the following received the most votes:

1. Egypt's Great Pyramids

2. The Taj Mahal, Agra, India

3. The Grand Canyon in Arizona

4. The Panama Canal

5. The Empire State Building, New York

6. St. Peter's Basilica, Rome

7. The Great Wall of China

While gathering the votes, the teacher noted that one student, a quiet girl, hadn't handed in her paper yet, so she asked the girl if she was having trouble with her list. The quiet girl replied, "Yes, a little. I couldn't quite make up my mind because there were so many."

The teacher said, "Well, tell us what you have, and maybe we can help."

The girl hesitated, then read, "I think the Seven Wonders of the World are:

1. To See

2. To Hear

3. To Touch

4. To Taste

5. To Feel

6. To Love

7. And to Belong."

The room was so quiet; you could have heard a pin drop.

In today's distracted world, it's very easy to forget this little girl's wisdom. Today I saw a TV advert for some technological toy. I call it a toy, they called it a 'necessity'. The advert told me not only did I need it, but in fact my life is not fulfilled because I don't yet own this product.

Then I saw a website ad. It told me that God wants me to be rich. Not only that, he wants me to get rich quickly. Of course, I had to buy someone's product first. Evidently, God wants them to get rich first...

Okay, they have made their point. Apparently without their stuff I am unimportant, and my life is destined to be mundane.

But then I get lucky and I hear another ad that promises to eliminate the mundane. According to the ad the mundane is something to be feared, and we can easily eliminate it.

I was at an event recently where people were sharing their opinions about life. One woman stood up and said, "Life is so... (she was struggling to find the right word) life is so ... daily." There's the problem. Life is so daily. No wonder we're easily tempted by one ad after another. We're trying to escape ordinary, daily life. And in our rush to avoid the mundane, we miss the miracles of the ordinary.

How do we find the miracles in ordinary life? I have found it starts with this simple sentence: "I never noticed that before." We have to remember how to wonder, or as the little girl said, how to see, hear, touch, smell, feel, love, and belong. When we do that, we get to delight in the wonders of the world that are right here, right now.

May this story serve as a gentle reminder to all of us that the things we overlook as simple and ordinary are often the most wonderful – and we don't have to travel anywhere special to experience them.

# 60

## WHAT WILL MATTER

*Poem by Michael Josephson (1942- )*
*American speaker and lecturer*

*R*eady or not, some day it will all come to an end.

There will be no more sunrises, no minutes, hours, or days.

All the things you collected, whether treasured or forgotten,
will pass to someone else.

Your wealth, fame, and temporal power will shrivel to
irrelevance.

It will not matter what you owned or what you were owed.

Your grudges, resentments, frustrations, and jealousies
will finally disappear.

So, too, your hopes, ambitions, plans,
and to-do lists will expire.

The wins and losses that once seemed so important
will fade away.

It will not matter where you came from
or what side of the tracks you lived on at the end.

It won't matter whether you were beautiful or brilliant.

Even your gender and skin colour will be irrelevant.

So what will matter? How will the value of your days
be measured?

What will matter is not what you bought but what you built;
not what you got but what you gave.

What will matter is not your success but your significance.

What will matter is not what you learned
but what you taught.

What will matter is every act of integrity, compassion,
courage, or sacrifice that enriched, empowered,
or encouraged others to emulate your example.

What will matter is not your competence but your character.

What will matter is not how many people you knew
but how many will feel a lasting loss when you're gone.

What will matter is not your memories
but the memories of those who loved you.

What will matter is how long you will be remembered,
by whom, and for what.

Living a life that matters doesn't happen by accident.

It's not a matter of circumstance but of choice.

Choose to live a life that matters.


Choose a better way to live...

*Barry*

# GRATITUDE

*I* would like to express my gratitude to all the people who have helped to make this book a reality.

Carola, my partner, thank you for your constant support and all the many hours spent reading and re-reading the skeleton of this book.

To my blog audience, without your prompting, there would be no book.

To all my customer friends, your support is why I write books.

Olivia, thank you for editing and supporting this book.

Zara, thank you for both proofreading and typesetting this book.

Clare, thank you for the cover design.

*L*ife is like a journey on a train with its stations, with changes of routes, and with accidents!

At birth, we boarded the train and met our parents, and we believe they will always travel on our side. However, at some station, our parents will step down from the train, leaving us on this journey alone. As time goes by, other people will board the train; and they will be significant i.e. our siblings, friends, children, and even the love of our life. Many will step down and leave a permanent vacuum. Others will go so unnoticed that we don't realise that they vacated their seats! This train ride will be full of joy, sorrow, fantasy, expectations, hellos, goodbyes, and farewells. Success consists of having a good relationship with all the passengers... requiring that we always give the best of ourselves.

The mystery to everyone is: we do not know at which station we ourselves will step down. So, we must live in the best way – love, forgive, and offer the best of who we are. It is important to do this because when the time comes for us to step down and leave our seat empty, we should leave behind beautiful memories for those who will continue to travel on the train of life without us.

I wish you a joyful journey for the coming years on your train of life. Reap success, give lots of love, and be happy.

More importantly, be thankful and enjoy the journey!

Lastly, I thank you for being one of the passengers on my train!